MW00852511

"I am so excited to have this book in my hands. As a biblical counselor, I eagerly await the opportunity to give this book to the parents of teenage boys. What they will be receiving is truly a treasure beyond price, not only for them but, more importantly, for their son and his future wife and children. The nuggets written here truly have the potential to change the world—the course of history. Over the past 30 years, I have witnessed the degeneration of manhood, and am thrilled Cliff has the heart to provide a tool for helping parents let boys see that the true path to manhood is the ultimate man, Jesus."

Bill Ewing
Former All American and professional baseball player
Co-founder of the International Association
of Biblical Counselors (IABC)

CALL ★ of ★ DUTY

CLIFF GRAHAM

CALL ★ of DUTY

SHOWING BOYS THE REAL JESUS

TATE PUBLISHING & *Enterprises*

Published by Tate Publishing & Enterprises, LLC
127 E. Trade Center Terrace | Mustang, Oklahoma 73064 USA
1.888.361.9473 | www.tatepublishing.com

Tate Publishing is committed to excellence in the publishing industry. The company reflects the philosophy established by the founders, based on Psalm 68:11,
"The Lord gave the word and great was the company of those who published it."

Book design copyright © 2008 by Tate Publishing, LLC. All rights reserved.
Cover design by Leah LeFlore
Interior design by Janae J. Glass
Illustrations by Jim O'Neal

Published in the United States of America

ISBN: 978-1-60696-452-1
1. Religion: Christianity: Christian Life- Boy's Issues
2. Christian Living: Spiritual Growth: Boy's Issues
08.11.05

FOR MY WIFE, CASSIE.
L.Y.H.B.

And for all the parents out there who just can't figure out their boy. Don't give up.

ACKNOWLEDGMENTS

This list would go on endlessly, so I will keep it just to the folks who directly influence our ministry and therefore this book:

Thank you, my Lord and Savior Christ Jesus.

My dad, Robert Graham, my hero, for being the warrior in my house, for giving me advice on life in the ministry, and showing me *the Call of Duty.*

My mom, Becki Graham, for protecting me from fiends and ensuring that I always knew love and joy in our home.

Holly, for being the funniest person I know and the best sister a guy could ask for.

Irene Graham and Jane Walker, the most wonderful grandmothers ever to walk the earth.

Ernie and Cindy Mecca, for letting me move their daughter to Texas.

Eric Mecca, for showing powerfully the compassionate side of Jesus, and for proving that mercy is part of *the Call of Duty.*

Jerry Smith, no one is irreplaceable but some are pretty close.

David Walker, for demonstrating Christ-like leadership on the front lines of ministry and letting us try all the crazy things we try.

Shirley Walker, for the help and advice while putting this book together.

Abbi Walker and Tina Dorrough, for picking up pizza boxes, planning food fights, crying with the girls, and showing them what an authentic pursuit of being a Godly woman looks like.

Bryan Yost, for being our resident skateboard/hard rock punk and creative genius, and Tara Yost, for stepping into the lives of "the fringe" as only you can.

Mackenzie Highland Ranch in Dubois, Wyoming, for letting us come up once a year and take over the place.

Todd Hillard, for showing me "Hang Out Theology" and encouraging me in my pursuit of the "craft."

Bill Ewing, for showing how much of an impact a coach can have on a young man's life.

A few other people who don't even know me but have been heavily influentail, namely Matt Chandler of The Village in Dallas, and Ravi Zacharias, men who keep me company on long runs by speaking into my earphones.

And to my wife Cassandra, thank you for the late night cookie baking, the critiquing, the joy of being a dad, the care of my household, and your wisdom and insight.

Finally, I want to give my heartfelt appreciation to the parents of the teenagers at the Alamo City Christian Fellowship, who have made a gigantic leap of faith in letting us try our unorthodox methods. This is your story. May the Lord Jesus bless it as He sees fit.

TABLE OF CONTENTS

FOREWORD

I should have known that if Cliff, an Army soldier and avid outdoorsman, was excited about going on the hike, I was in over my head. Our families were vacationing together in the mountains, and I watched Cliff eagerly stuffing food, gear, and two one-gallon jugs of water in his pack. He was exhorting our family that this was indeed a trek that would be worthy of our time. Forget the fact that it was our first day in 7,000+ feet of altitude and I am 25 years his senior. He has a commander's persona and enthusiasm that can muster adventure in the most timid of troops.

So conquer the summit of Lone Peak in Montana we must. From the top of the gondola we would hike four miles and nearly 3,000 feet to the top, risking our shins and ankles on loose shale that spanned much of the climb. An hour and a half into our ascent, hands on hips and sucking for air that seemed to evaporate before it hit my lungs, I noticed that we had lost sight of our leader. I was trailing way behind, dragging my feet and knowing I was too far in to go back down, too far out to find fresh resolve.

If that wasn't enough, my husband, middle child, and I were precariously perched on what is lovingly referred to as "The Blade." This 50-yard stretch of rock near the summit is

30 inches wide and has a 1,000-foot drop on either side. Sanity hit, I realized I could slip and die, so I froze in fear and started adding up what was in my savings account that would pay for a helicopter rescue. My family finally coaxed me across the Blade, crawling on hands and knees to the other side.

So what does this have to do with *Call of Duty?* Everything. As a mother of a teenage son, I know that I'm in over my head. One minute life is a nice walk on a sunny day, the next I am precariously perched on a ledge clinging for dear life. The little boy whose chubby fingers grabbed my hand to cross the street now grins down at me, engaging in activities that could potentially claim his life, *and I am supposed to be okay with this?*

I have found Cliff's words refreshingly relevant to where I walk as a mom. He gives practical insight into the heart of my son, helping me better understand how he thinks and how I can best relate to him. His words have brought about course corrections in my parenting style. But most importantly, his work has stirred my heart to climb again—to believe God for the highest and best for my son and for my relationship with him.

The premise of *Call of Duty* is to challenge a boy for action, and in reading its pages, this mom has found a voice to do so.

by Shirley Walker
Author of *Window in a Glass House*

ON "THURTING" AND WARRIORS

"Most men live lives of quiet desperation, and go to the grave with the song still in them."

—Henry David Thoreau

You know it's a new world when even the spit wad undergoes a technological revolution. I had it explained to me at a retreat not long ago by a young man who was eager to demonstrate his prowess at annoying people. Apparently all you have to do is break off the end of a ballpoint pen, stuff a few air soft pellets (small plastic bb's) into your mouth, lock on to your target, and then spray it with the pellets. It's called "thurting" because of the sound the pellets make when they leave the tube. The principle is exactly the same as it was in the old days, but the look is different. Kind of like other things in life.

Okay, maybe your son isn't the one who actually does the thurting. Perhaps he's the one who watches and laughs. Maybe he's the one who looks around to see if they're all in trouble. Maybe he's the one getting thurted. Whoever he is, he struggles with the same issues and problems that boys have struggled with since the invention of the boy.

We demand ten steps to success in our culture, double-click it and then forget it. Fixing kids ought to be the same. You should, in the brave new world of technology and forward-thinking, be able to order a patch for your son's soul as easily as a latte at Starbucks. Be careful, though. Anyone claiming to be an expert on teenagers is probably selling you an advice manual. Those books are the hottest new thing in our culture, and they're all various forms of the same message: *This* guy has the answer. It might be the seven steps to lose those last few pounds, or the nine steps to follow in order to retire to a castle in the south of France by age 34.

For raising teenagers, there's usually some guy with a fancy degree that plunges into the depths of the psyche in order to eloquently tell you something that sounds just smart enough to convince you to buy his next book. We'll call him the Ten Step Solution Guy. All troubles with your moody teenage son go away forever once you do steps 1–10. By saying certain words at certain times using certain slang, your kid will think you're just as cool as all his buddies. A valiant effort, to be sure, and the irony of me writing a book while criticizing books is duly noted.

The problem with this approach is that it's kind of like fighting the Hydra, the mythical monster that kept growing heads when they were cut off. Just when you think you've figured out the coolest, most relevant way to confront your offspring about his endlessly sagging pants, that indecisive hydra called Style issues an edict. *"No longer are the pants to be sagged,"* Style proclaims, *"they are to be 4 sizes too small, and they must be pants normally worn by the opposite gender."* All teenagers, even those who think they are individuals and buck the trends, submit to Style. Someone eventually comes along, cuts off that head, and another one sprouts again.

Ten Step Solution Guy might have forgotten that at one point he was a teenager as well. So were you. Don't get me wrong; I'm not saying there hasn't been brilliant work done by experts in the field of parenting. Books can be terrific tools. I quote the Old Smart Guys (hereafter referred to as OSG's) regularly because truth is timeless. But isn't it usually the case that when you ask a set of parents how their kids turned out so well, they just sort of shrug their shoulders and say, "I dunno"?

If they claim it was because they followed the proper instructions, then how do you explain parents doing the exact same things unsuccessfully? Parents have enormous influence over the fate of their kids, but when you get right down to it teens eventually have to make their own decisions, be they wise ones or poor ones. As much as you may wish to, following them around throughout life won't be possible.

There you are, trying once again on Sunday morning to wake your son up in order to go to church, and he just ... doesn't ... want ... to.

No amount of pleading matters. Eventually he caves in to your demands but only because you're threatening him with the grounding-du-jour. Maybe you had to bribe him with the promise of a Pop Tart at the breakfast table, or a burrito after the service. Either way, he always seems to shrug off talk about Jesus. So what's a concerned parent to do?

Boys, like all the rest of us, need to discover who the *real* Jesus is. Not the Jesus of Hollywood or the Jesus of religion, but the actual man that we read about in the Scriptures. The

One who doesn't just make gentle requests but issues orders in the heat of battle.

Many advice books have been written about Christianity, but somehow a lot of boys are still missing it. Partly because no teenager I know of reads advice books. It falls on you, the parents, to help him get a glimpse of the authentic Jesus. The Jesus of love, life, danger, excitement ... and war.

The "war" I am referring to isn't necessarily military combat. Those are the least important wars we fight, and I say that as an Army officer in active status. The war is in homes, marriages, schools, and offices. Some of the bravest battlefield warriors in history were complete cowards in their personal lives. What happens on a battlefield is temporary; what happens between a man and his family resonates forever.

Being physically brave is a large part of it, but that makes no difference if you can't even hold the devotion of one woman. As the prophet Jeremiah lamented, "If **you** have raced with men on foot and they have worn **you** out, how can **you** compete with horses? If **you stumble** in safe country, how will **you** manage in the thickets by the Jordan?"(Jeremiah 12:5).

In ancient times a young man was given one option: become a warrior. There weren't self-help manuals and group hug sessions back in the old days. He could figure out later what type of tradesmen he would be, but it was much more important to first develop his ability to fight wars. Because that's what he was. Built for war.

Everything else in life centered on his ability to cope with stress, make tough decisions, and never give up. It doesn't matter what time period is at hand, all young men are wired the same. They feel *alive* and worth something when they're called to duty. They feed off of people depending on them. They give everything they have to do the right thing, and that's only developed by warrior training.

One of the hats I put on for my work is that of a soldier, and I can testify that no soldier is created overnight through a ten step program. It requires pain, tears, sweat, anger, determination, violence, and unrelenting courage. And that's just the initial training, never mind fighting wars. Yet despite the fact that misery haunts you every day of soldier preparation, a man never feels as alive as when he is calling forth every ounce of his internal fire to finish the mission.

It relates directly to why boys no longer care about going to church and look bored when you try to tell them about Jesus: there isn't enough war. The feminizing of boys in the culture is at full steam, and many do it with good intentions. It's very important to encourage mercy and compassion. So by using all this inflammatory language about the glory of warfare, I'm not suggesting we should desire it day and night. It's more like a preparation. You can ignore the fight, observe the fight, or join the fight. The choice is yours. There is no middle ground.

A boy eventually becomes a man, and in order for that process to be more than biological evolution he needs to develop the heart of a warrior. Only then will he stand strong in his faith when confronted with assaults on his marriage, children, and livelihood.

I am not a parent of teenagers (yet), and after observing all that I have so far, I'm honestly nervous about it. So I don't want to hand down parenting advice any more than a ballet dancer could lecture a submarine captain. This isn't a parenting manual. It doesn't offer profound insight into the raising of teenagers. It doesn't cite a dozen studies by men wearing spectacles at universities. I don't speak with the authority of one who successfully raised half a dozen boys to manhood and they're now all doctors, lawyers, and preachers.

I do, however, hang out with teenage boys for a living, and I've talked with a lot of other guys who do so as well. We've had the same conversations with parents a dozen times. We've all come to the same observation: many young men don't care about spiritual things because there's no *Call of Duty*.

Of all the stuff I have seen thrown at youth pastors and parents, there doesn't seem to be any substitute for communicating, in a relevant way, the manly call to arms that Jesus provides. One day that goofy teenager with pimples will be a man, and he'll look back on his "training" years in your house for answers to life's challenges. Will he remember a list of 1,000 things *not* to do in order to be right with God? Or will he remember the warrior influence that led him to hear *the Call*?

Think of this as being like a piece of intelligence received by decoders. You are the commanding general. The battle is raging, and someone whispers something in your ear. An encoded message has been sent to you from the front lines, carried by a messenger who's in the thick of it daily.

Your troops are communicating to you how they are doing, what the status of their supply is, what the enemy is throwing at them, and how they had to adjust. It doesn't make a whole lot of sense from your vantage point, but then again you aren't on the front lines. You were once, a while ago. But back then it was ... different.

You have the authority to simply demand obedience from your men, but you remember how it felt when someone was always telling you what to do without trying to·understand exactly where your foxhole was. This information doesn't give you the entire plan of action to take next, but it does help you make better, more informed decisions. You nod your head at the messenger and then push on.

So this is for you parents, youth workers, and teachers who work with boys. Mostly it's for the parents. Some of it may offend previously held ideas, though that is not my intent. Quite the opposite, it is composed in love by someone who truly thinks the world of you, joyfully dreads having your job, and just wants to throw you a bit of info that might help you speak to your kid about the meaning of life. I think you'll find that a dispatch from the foxhole is what finally helps the whole battlefield make a little more sense.

This book is written loosely in the style of the two main formats for military orders: the warning order and the operations order. Part 1 is the warning order and it is designed to give you a head's up on what your boy's world is and the influences he faces.

In part 2 are the operation orders, which define more clearly the situation, the mission, and the execution of that mission. Remember, they're only suggestions and not fail-safe solutions. I have also noticed that boys like really manly quotes and Bible verses, so a few of those are tossed in as well. At the end you will find an appendix that addresses some questions a parent (moms in particular) might have upon reading this book. Men, a lot of what you will encounter here you have heard/read/seen before, but I have made an attempt to translate a lot of that masculine journey type stuff into the language of the modern teenager.

Jesus told a lot of stories to illustrate his points, and so will I, though I've altered the specifics of whom or what each story I tell involves. No real names, except those adults who have given their permission. There aren't any illustrations that would compromise anyone's privacy. The idea is not to highlight any one person but to see some consistent patterns. The heart can be communicated without personal details, and the themes are pretty universal.

Maybe you're a single mom at the end of her rope. Perhaps you're a dad who can't figure out why the kid won't try harder. Whoever you are, hang tough. Your son knows you love him if you're giving maximum effort. The next step might simply be saying things in such a way that the flames of war are lit inside of him.

The ancient war poet Heraclitus once wrote, "Out of every 100 men on a battlefield; 80 are worthless, 10 are just targets, 9 are true fighters, and one is a warrior. It is the warrior who brings the others back."

All of the fatherless children and abandoned wives prove that we have plenty of worthless targets.

We need more warriors.

PART ★ ONE

NATURE OF THE BEAST

...be strong, therefore, and show yourself a man.

1 Kings 2:2

The vans ground to a halt in the darkness of 9:45 p.m. I sat still in the driver's seat and waited to see what would happen. Whenever teenagers are in a confined vehicle for any amount of time, they engage in two activities. The first is listening to someone's music player by sharing headphones with them, and the second is shouting over the music in their ears. I have yet to see any of them figure out that simply removing the earphones from one's head is more than sufficient for carrying on a conversation with a buddy in the seat in front of them. They haven't reached the age where you realize volume doesn't necessarily mean clarity.

In the two-hour drive from the church to the retreat center, what was once a perfectly clean 15-passenger van had become a traveling carnival. Chocolate, crackers, and cotton candy (don't ask) were firmly imbedded into the carpet. I've often wondered why it was so urgent to bring junk food along only to leave half of it on the floor. Even in such a short amount of time, and before we had even begun the retreat, the smell was enough to kill young goats or small children.

Finally, one brilliant young man clear in the back seat realized that we were no longer moving.

"Hey, what's going on? Are we here yet?"

I didn't say a word, quietly gathered my stuff, and exited the vehicle.

"Dude, Cliff, what's going on? When's dinner?"

"You already had dinner, bro. You're on your own now," I replied.

I walked away from their confused faces and stopped by the van where Tina, one of our youth staff members, was doing the exact same thing. Only this time, I got to see just how different an experience driving girls can be. Sure, there's laughing and giggling, but one notices the general lack of earsplitting volume and horrendous smell.

"Tina, is this where we're staying?"

Tina replied, "No idea. Everyone's on their own."

The girls, a little confused, looked at one another.

I glanced back toward the guys' van (we had separated them on purpose to see what would happen). Everyone was outside and beginning to engage in various forms of mischief. Four of them had already sprinted toward the darkest part of the forest and disappeared.

A few more were running in and out of the meeting center, chasing one another with handfuls of pebbles. Only two of them looked as though they had any concern for the wellbeing of their luggage. They stared at me, waiting for my usual booming voice to start bringing order out of the chaos.

The girls were busy trying to find their sleeping bags and organize their nesting area for the weekend. Some had unpacked quickly and were disappearing at the same rate as the guys, but for the most part they were still sifting.

Some conversations among the girls had already broken out regarding what *exactly* it was that so-and-so had told such-and-such at the party last Friday night, and whether thus-and-thus knew anything about it.

Abbi, the girls' director, walked out of the cabin and started giving orders to the kids. I touched her shoulder and said, "Remember, no instructions of any kind."

"Oh yeah, almost forgot."

I could tell that Abbi, the most Type A of all the staff, was fretting about lawsuits and liabilities as our youth group began to resemble a pack of baboons being attacked by fire ants.

The theme for the weekend was "Anarchy." It goes without saying that this was a tough sell for many parents, but our reasoning was simple: we wanted to show the students how order and design are so important to our lives. Too much freedom can actually become bondage. Living under the design God has placed in creation leads to the most satisfaction.

We wanted to show them what would happen if there were no rules or structure of any kind. They would be excited at first, but then realize that no one was cooking them meals or planning activities.

That's all well and good when you're pitching the idea to the elders, but in practical application things can get sketchy. As the old saying goes, no battle plan survives first contact with the enemy.

One of our young men called out, "Cliff, you gotta check

out this spider; he's bigger than my shoe and hisses when you come near him!"

"No he doesn't, liar! He isn't bigger than camel spiders in Korea. My brother said that camel spiders are two feet tall and get their name because they can kill and eat camels," came a reply from the darkness.

I made my way into the guys' section of the conference cabin we had rented for the weekend. There were about 50 bunk beds that had been firmly bolted to the floor. The owners clearly knew what would happen if anything wasn't. I found myself staring at what looked to be an exact reenactment of the Battle of the Alamo built out of mattresses from the bunks.

There was Davy Crockett in the corner, swinging a pillow instead of Old Betsy. Yonder was Jim Bowie bravely stabbing people with a bag of Cheetoh's. Artillery support was being provided by a young man "thurting" the incoming troops (see the introduction for a description of thurting).

Some of the kids were starting to notice that I hadn't said a single word yet. Others didn't care.

"So what's supposed to be happening?"

"Where's the food?"

"Tell Derek to stop taking my chips!"

After an hour or so, I walked back outside to track down the mass of bodies that had departed for the river. Hey, I'm willing to experiment, but I'm not crazy. Explaining to a mother that her son had drowned as a result of my innovative new youth ministry techniques would be rough going.

The moon was at full harvest, and a soft breeze blew past my ears as I made my way through the forest. I could hear the sound of the water as it babbled along the rocks, straining my ears to catch any laughter or shouting that would indicate the correct direction to take.

Through the trees I could see a glow. I knew some of the kids had brought with them flashlights, so I made my way toward it. I didn't want to announce my presence since my goal was to observe them in their natural habitat, kind of like how *National Geographic* photographers hide out waiting to capture a photo of animals fighting or engaging in mating rituals. Hopefully none of that was going on.

As I approached, the conversations became more audible. Instead of the laughter and crude talk that I was expecting to hear, only one person was speaking at a time and in quiet tones. Utilizing all of the stealth I could muster, I crept up to a tree on the riverbank just a few yards away from the kids and wasn't prepared for what I saw.

They had taken all of their flashlights and lanterns and made a makeshift campfire out of them. There were about a dozen of them, both guys and girls, sitting around this "campfire" sharing their stories.

As I sat there, still as possible in the quiet darkness, I heard each young person pouring their hearts out to the others in the group. There were stories of fathers who had abandoned their families, stories of mothers who were self-destructing, stories of abuse, heartache, and yearning.

These weren't the typical teenage self-centered accounts of how unfair life was because a girlfriend broke up with you. It was genuinely anguishing to listen to, and as each one took their turn, I noticed something else.

The young man facilitating the discussion was the last

person I would have expected. He had a torrid background, involved in drugs and gangs. This was typical of the kids we have in our ministry, but he was especially rough around the edges. He liked hanging around all of us, despite his admitting that God was just some vague concept to him.

His own story came out, shockingly candid. When he finished he was encouraging all the others to open up more, showing leadership and trying to fix problems. Some of them didn't have electrifying tales of woe, but all were honest.

The night air was getting chilly, but the shivers I was experiencing weren't from the weather. This had been unannounced, unprovoked, unguided, and would have not occurred under any other circumstance.

If we had done the usual thing where there is a timeline and that timeline is to be followed at all costs, we would have missed it. I wish I could say there was mass revival that night. I wish I could point out that my hard work in preparing a message about order and design had been the instigation of it.

Instead I was left with God once again showing me that He stubbornly moves in the least expected ways. Sure, I had a talk with them all about sneaking away in a co-ed group, but it was hard to get too upset after what I had witnessed.

It's great to experience a spontaneous hour-long prayer time, but sometimes we might just step back and watch events unfold. Doing so reminds us that God is in control, despite how well-planned life is. Anarchy normally means disorder and chaos, but in this instance it resulted in complete honesty and openness. No disorder whatsoever. The boy who had been leading the campfire counseling session eventually came to know Jesus as his savior, but it was not an easy process and required the use of many unorthodox methods. He did not kneel and say the "sinner's prayer" during the last session of that retreat, but Christ had pricked his heart and was beginning to do a work in his life from that moment on. Thankfully, the Lord was around that flashlight campfire.

In order to maintain sanity during Wednesday night services, I sometimes tell our students that they're not special and unique snowflakes. When trying to move mass quantities of undisciplined teens from point A to point B, the last thing I tend to be concerned about is their self-esteem.

In reality, teens couldn't be more unique. The fellow who tries to wrap all young people into blanket assumptions is being foolish, so while I tease the kids about not being unique, it's important to note their individual personalities as God created them.

Here are the six main personality categories that I have noticed among boys. They aren't exhaustive; no kid perfectly fits any of these molds. They do tend to lean one direction more than the others, though. Read each description carefully, and you will probably be able to see the recipe that makes up your own teen. In each category there will always be an Alpha Male. Every one of these cliques has a ringleader, the guy calling all the shots. It is the Alpha Male who naturally separates himself from the other boys.

Let's get on our safari gear, grab a camera, and observe the "nature of the beast" of those strange creatures we call "boys." I will mention some possible ways to talk about God with them in the last chapter, but here's a glimpse into their world...

★ THE JOCK

This kid has a lot going for him. Popular at school, he has accumulated a vast number of female admirers as evidenced by his large fan club in the stands. A Jock is very friendly and would be able to charm money out of the bank.

He usually has a laid-back personality. The default leader of any group, charisma will never be a problem for him. He's the one who makes the funniest wisecracks and usually gets his way. The girls all want him, the guys all want to be him. Even those who pretend they don't. A natural byproduct of his excellence is an inflated ego, though he may disguise it well.

The Alpha Male of this group is either the captain of the squad or the star quarterback. Other athletes on the team will do their best to get noticed by him since he is in charge of getting the ball to people.

When I was in junior high, there was a kid named Jason who was the undisputed king of the locker room. You just didn't mess with him. He was awesome at basketball, he was awesome at football, he was awesome at every single thing he ever tried, and it drove all of us crazy. We were in awe of him, but we also couldn't stand him.

I remember feeling resentful when all the girls would run up to Jason in the hallway between classes. He had to literally climb over a herd of giggling females in order to reach his locker. Jason was a friendly guy and never gave us any reason to dislike him personally. It's just a fact of life that whoever sits on top of the hill is the one everyone is gunning for. The Jock loves to have a good time and might be found at the nearest party after the game Friday night. Other guys will show up at the same party to be seen near him. The hope is that any girls the Jock doesn't want might take an interest in them. It's exactly like something on the Discovery Channel.

The Jock usually has a father who pushes him hard. If they have a loving relationship, the father and son will embrace no matter the outcome of the game. If he believes that his dad only loves him for how good he is, there is true agony in his defeats. If he doesn't have a father in the home, I've noticed that the coach of his sports team serves as that figure, whether he wants to or not.

He's just as skilled at playing the church game as he is the football field. The elderly ladies are charmed, and the men are pleased that the boy "seems to have a good head on his shoulders." This could be completely genuine … or not.

The good news is that most campus Bible study leaders and youth group student leaders are Jocks. They also tend to lead Fellowship of Christian Athletes (FCA) huddle groups, which have an enormous influence on the schools. FCA employees have told me countless stories of how a stellar athlete becoming a Christian or leading an FCA "huddle" (sort of like a mini youth group) had a significant impact on their team. In rural areas, like most of Texas and all of Wyoming, the leader of the sports team wields an influence similar to a politician. If he is a follower of Christ, many in the community will see it and pay attention.

★ THE PHILOSOPHER

This is the kid who believes he has the answers to all of the world's pesky problems. Usually concerned with bucking all fashion trends and molds, he fits perfectly into the mold of fashion trend-buckers.

He isolates himself a lot but hangs around other like-minded people. He's fascinated by fantasy and loves darkness. Because of this, people might assume he's into gothic activities or worships Satan. He overanalyzes things to an extreme and can completely baffle you with the depths of his laziness. Yes, Mom, even walking to the fridge to get his *own* soda is too much work. The yard will rarely be mowed on time if it's his assigned chore.

Physical exertion of any kind is avoided, unless he is trying to become a nature-loving hippie to impress the nature-loving hippie girls. In that case he may suddenly take up mountain biking or randomly explain to you at the dinner table the value of hiking in the woods to alleviate stress. I once led a youth group hike to the top of a mountain with the assistance of my brother-in-law, who was shocked to see that the reason some of the kids were struggling was because they were attempting to haul books about philosophy (written by semi-stoned beat poets) up to the peak in order to better connect with the "spirit of creativity." The inflated sense of genius is absolutely typical of these clowns. Remember, *only they* have ever truly thought about world hunger or the dangers of greed, and *if the world only listened to them*, all of these troubles would disappear as quickly as hot cookies on your kitchen counter.

Most sentences out of the Philosopher's mouth are laced with sarcasm. Eye rolling is another common symptom, and he rarely applies himself to anything that's not a videogame. He's the kid who scoffs down his nose at the jock and forms discussion groups and internet chat rooms to talk about how lame jocks are, and how best to use the Sword of Destiny to defeat Grimlog the Terrible in whatever version of his favorite fantasy game is out that month.

The Alpha Male of this group could be one of two species. The first is that he is the outcast of all the outcasts. He'll wear the most shocking clothing and say the most outlandish things. The other kids are amazed that he doesn't seem to care what anyone thinks. His teachers are amazed that his parents don't make him shower once in a while.

The second is that he maintains good personal hygiene but is deeply consumed with all things dark. He loves to explore morbid things and has a love of angry music. He will pull in likeminded kids who aren't really troubled but like the thought of rebelling so that girls who like rebels will pay attention to them.

The Philosopher is pretty sullen most of the time. He can be friendly when it suits him. There are plenty of girls who are attracted to this, so he might have a girlfriend with similar interests. The relationship can be very serious and last a long time, since the two of them are bonded by common problems and see themselves as outcasts.

He sits quietly at night when he's alone, secretly wondering why his shoulders aren't broader and his arms aren't stronger. Disappearing into a virtual world over the internet or in videogames is much more appealing to him than going to church, where people usually look at his dark clothing and facial piercings with disgust.

★ THE MOODY MUSICIAN

This is the rock star of the group. He has copied the hair and clothing style of some popular-for-the-moment band on MTV. It might be baggy pants. It might be tight pants. It might be women's pants. Either way, there is a statement he is trying to make to everyone. That statement usually is, "You all don't understand the demons I struggle with in my head, so shut up and listen to my tortured lyrics and angry guitar riffs."

The musician has either (1) started a rock band, or (2) has been invited to join one and refused, claiming that he was too busy starting his *own* rock band, and he doesn't need your stupid rock band because *his* rock band is going to sell 8 gazillion records, so there.

The girls who hang around him are swooned by his devil-may-care attitude and tortured lyrics with angry guitar riffs. He also pretends that he doesn't want to be the Jock and writes songs about it. Most of these songs contain lyrics that rant about how Jocks are phony, but if magically given broad shoulders and amazing athletic ability, I'm convinced the Moody Musician would drop those songs pretty quickly and sing instead about how awesome football is. I don't say that to knock them; I'm just coming from many conversations with them that led me to conclude they, like all boys, secretly envy the Jock.

Don't confuse the Moody Musician with the kid who just likes to strum on the guitar, because nearly all boys dream of being in a rock band. The Moody Musician is the one who has become obsessed with the culture of the musician. Because he is always looking for creative inspiration, he's very emotional. He likes to brag about how his band is playing multiple venues this weekend, although he doesn't mention that those venues are his buddy's backyard party. Once in a while, there is a true breakout success story from these ranks, but as they age, most boys tend to grow out of Moody Musician phase.

I am not denying the musical talent that your teen might have in any way. Some of these kids are truly amazing with a guitar or drum set, and what sounds to you like a rabid cat locked in a trashcan is actually a very complex musical arrangement. My mom is a gifted music teacher and disagrees wholeheartedly with me on this one. Some of the stuff I listened to when I was growing up did indeed sound like Mr. Mittens locked in the trashcan, but it connected with me like it somehow connects with your son. The most frequent reason given is that it sounds "real."

The great irony is that country music, and not rabid-cat-in-a-trashcan music, is actually closer to real life than musicians want to admit. Not all of us struggle with voices in our heads or hatred of capitalism, but we *have* owned a really great pickup truck. We *have* owned a loyal dog. We *have* been really mad at our significant other and told them so. I just described roughly 87 percent of all country music. But I digress. What I am trying to help you understand is the subculture that has developed among guys who have easy access to instruments and watch MTV a lot.

Their view of the entire world is seen through a lens stuffed with drama and moodiness, as with most creative people. Of course, such people have had names like Beethoven and Michelangelo, so maybe that isn't always a bad thing. Bluntly speaking, you can't encourage them to like any style of music that they don't like. If they hate Christian music, it isn't necessarily because it's Christian—they just don't like the music. They tend to think that their parents want them to abandon all sense of individuality and therefore give up what they feel sets them apart. Did I mention they were moody?

★ THE KNUCKLEHEAD

That's the affectionate nick-name I have given this boy. He's smart but usually doesn't act like it. He has boundless energy, is consumed with finding that next hilarious thing to do, is constantly in motion, and will visibly twitch if you try to calm him down. "I'm bored" comes out of his mouth several times a day.

He functions on comedy. Video clips of people falling down or doing stupid things are the equivalent of intellectual stimulation for him. He has the ability to focus for about 1 ½ minutes and then laughs at the funny thing that just happened over there.

Knucklehead has a love of destroying things, and fire is an endless fascination for him. When I was in my youth (not that long ago), I was a major Knucklehead in this area. Burning little piles of grass all over the yard nearly drove my poor mother to insanity.

One particular episode took place my senior year of high school. Some buddies called me up on the phone one evening and said, "Dude, you gotta come out to Adam's so we can burn stuff!" That sounded more exciting than watching TV, so I drove to a friend's house out in the country. As I pulled up, three of my closest pals were holding giant red containers full of fuel. It was a gathering of the biggest doofuses you can fathom, and we were entirely unsupervised by a responsible third party.

Our strategic vision was to pour gasoline down the concrete drainage ditch that bordered the driveway. It was easily forty feet long, the perfect place to create the River of Fire. I can still remember the excitement when the match was struck and held over a glittering cascade of gasoline. It never occurred to us that this might be dangerous; we only cared that it was gonna be *awesome!*

It was awesome indeed, as the flames roared to a height of twenty feet. It looked like something in a movie about explorers escaping a lost jungle temple. The River of Fire was everything we hoped it would be. Problem was the Einstein who poured the fuel out hadn't put the bucket back down, so flames raced into the container.

Visions of atomic fury shot through my mind as I dove for cover. Fortunately the explosion never came, although my friend's mother had her entire rose garden destroyed. These are the kinds of things that Knuckleheads do: have fun at all costs.

Some will diagnose this kid with Attention Deficit Disorder, and since I'm not a physician, I can accept that. However, sometimes he just needs a chance to run it out and not another shot of Ritalin. If given the proper place to channel their energy, Knuckleheads can be the hardest workers in the group. At a camp once I saw that one of our many resident Knuckleheads was causing more trouble than he was productivity, so I sent him off to a small rock pit that was on the mountainside nearby. I informed him that we needed the pathway between buildings to be marked better, and he was the only one I could count on to get the job done. Sure enough, not more than half an hour elapsed before the path was completed.

For a Knucklehead, sitting through a church service is considered to be punishment. Sitting through Sunday school *and* a church service is relentless torture. It's got nothing to do with the quality of the message or the style of the worship; he just has a hard time paying attention to anything that does not involve the assembling of explosives or the whacking of heads with objects.

In church, all pieces of paper in the seatbacks within reaching distance, such as offering envelopes and Welcome Visitor cards, will be written on, torn up, and spit-wadded long before the preacher reaches his second point of the sermon.

No amount of pleading ever seems to work; this kid just doesn't really care about spiritual matters except at a time of his own choosing. He's the one who will ask the dumb question to get a laugh, get distracted by ants on the floor, and then surprise the heck out of you in a sudden moment of seriousness.

★ THE GANGSTER

This fellow somewhat resembles the Jock, except for the fact that his clothing style changes frequently, depending on which gangster rap artist is popular that month, which makes him a little bit Moody Musician as well. He is charismatic, charming, and has a tough edge in his eye. He tends to be possessive. He treats his friends with a callous attitude and has a love of unlawful things. He might not be an actual gang member, but he holds a fascination of them.

One of my jobs in the Army was to serve as a military police officer. I had the chance to work with a lot of guys who were civilian cops and brought a wealth of experience to the table when dealing with gangs. I learned from them that much of the gang culture among high school kids is about image: there's a lot more talk than actual action.

Please don't misunderstand me on this one. I am in no way downplaying the enormous trouble that a kid gets into when he joins a gang. It's a terrible brew when you mix violence with ego. The point I am trying to make is that if your son hasn't already gotten into trouble with the police, chances are he is still experimenting. He might be wearing strange color arrangements or using language that sounds nothing like English. He's in a precarious place, but just because he has acquired some strange new clothing, all is not lost. The deadly gangs that play with real bullets and knives await him if he gets too far into this phase, but for the most part he is testing the waters.

The Gangster feels the need to prove his manliness in everything. He embellishes stories of his misdeeds in order to get attention. There might be some remorse over things he has done, but it's a slippery slope back to the old ways. Girls love him, and guys try to be like him.

The Alpha Male Gangster is the shot-caller. He's worked his way to the top and has a vested interest in remaining there. Girls are attracted to him because he displays all the traits of masculinity that other boys don't: leadership, protection, and loyalty. The problem is that all of the traits have been contaminated with selfishness. Instead of upholding the weak and defending the helpless, he's in it for himself.

Violent emotions can burst out of Gangsters at any time. This can be fueled by substance abuse, or it could just be the pain of unseen wounds. Fatherless boys are naturally the most susceptible to this. He usually hides his turmoil behind the tough guy mask, but I continue to be delighted at the refreshing honesty that comes from these guys. They flat-out tell you exactly what they are thinking at any given moment. We can get right to the meat of a discussion without wasting time with too much chit-chat.

He's usually itching to prove to me how tough he is. Sometimes I give them the chance to try and take me down, but my 240-pound frame and rigorous combat training allows me to prevail in wrestling matches pretty easily. I do this to show them that if they always walk around with a chip on their shoulder, someone much tougher than them is going to deliver quite a bit of pain to their body. If I were to attack a man who outweighed me by a hundred pounds and was trained to kill, pain therapy would be applied to me as well. Life Lessons 101, if you will.

It's tough to pinpoint what a Gangster's reaction to church will be. It might be a boring activity that he does in order to appease his mom, or he might construct a bizarre attachment to religious ritual and translate that into gang culture. Some of the most brutal gang members in a prison will have tattoos of Jesus on the cross. Maybe they like dramatic irony or something.

Probably the most consistent reaction I have witnessed is the lack of respect for "posers," people who say one thing and do another. Gangsters have a hard time understanding the concept of grace, so they don't realize that Christians remaining sinners is normal. They live in a world where respect is king, and posers aren't even worthy of the bottom rung. But if you are up front about who you are and what you want from them, they have a remarkable amount of tolerance for you. They crave being treated like a man and feeling like you respect them.

I was hanging out with a Gangster once who told me that he believed "all this Jesus stuff was real." The word "stuff" was substituted with something else, but you get the picture. He also told me to "keep it gangsta," his way of saying that the message needed to be authentic, not covered in excessive religion. In a later chapter I will talk about what "excessive religion" means. For our purposes here I will just emphasize once more that authenticity and bluntness are the languages of the streets.

Gansters typically don't want to come to church, so you have to go to them in their neighborhood, where they feel like they are in control.

★ THE MELTING POT

Melting Pot is the boy who is fairly good at a lot of stuff but not *great* at anything. He can make the team but doesn't do anything special while on it. He makes decent grades, some sub-jects better than others. He's had a girlfriend or two.

There's nothing you'd notice about him, and that's the point: he's simply not exceptional. American culture demands exceptional, and this kid just kind of…lives. He has buddies, likes to laugh, and enjoys his family. I call him Melting Pot because he'll usually be the sidekick to one of the guys mentioned above. He might go through all the categories during high school, sometimes in the same week.

Let me throw another type of boy into this category: the lifelong churchgoer whose parents have been bringing him since he was a baby. It might be that he has been home schooled or has gone through a Christian academy his entire life. His experiences outside this environment have been limited, and it shows by the awkwardness he feels around his peers. He probably will tell you that he has a hard time making friends in the youth group, and it's because he hasn't had a chance to develop the teen social skills that the others are forced to employ daily.

Melting Pots seem to be good kids with a lot going for them. Their biggest advantage is that they usually have a very close family and benefit from the love that comes from such an environment. Their biggest obstacle is that they have been sheltered and believe being a Christian means hiding from Lost Kids.

The reason I include them here is that they might not have started to experience the angst of the teen years quite yet, and you're unsure which path they will be drawn to. They might even watch in shock as the rest of their peers in the youth group do things that aren't "Christian."

The one thing I can say with a fair amount of certainty is that, as they grow up, they'll start to gravitate in one direction or the other. They won't remain the same as they are now because the world will eventually confront them. And like it or not, they're more aware of the world than you may think.

Any friend with internet access or an iPod is the Worldview Mailman making a delivery into your son's brain.

The teenager in your life is a mixture of several options above. He might be one part Jock and two parts Melting Pot. Perhaps he is part Melting Pot and half Moody Musician. No matter how you shake them up, there are a few things they all have in common, which I will now cover.

CHAOS AND CONFLICT
(AND SOCKS)

As I pointed out in the bunk bed story, the first common trait among boys is the genetic desire to destroy things. For the Knucklehead, any arrangement of any kind must be dis-arranged immediately. Since the sheer amount of things that boys want to lose/kill/destroy would fill an entire volume on its own, I will focus on socks.

If mom has packed socks in the dresser drawer, then the socks must be de-drawered. Socks are the endangered species of a boy's dresser, especially on trips. I collect an average of 10 pairs of them per retreat weekend. Summer camp provides enough socks to warm the feet of an entire Third World village. The most remarkable part of this phenomenon is that they never seem to run out. It's as if they bring along extra pairs with the explicit goal of losing them.

The family dinner table is a terrific example of this. Assuming that you actually have everyone together for once, just notice how the boys will completely disregard the orderly way in which mom laid things out and plow right in. Perhaps eager young mothers will spruce up their meals with parsley and little sauce bowls, but as time goes on, they tend to surrender to the inevitable and just provide food in whatever container will hold it.

Interestingly, creating chaos is not the goal, because hardwired into them is the desire to rebuild what they've destroyed. Let's go back to the Anarchy retreat. Upon entering the room, all of the mattresses were immediately torn down. Once they had been removed from their place of origin, the next act was to construct something out of them. The Lord promised Adam in Genesis 3 that he would only eat crops after sweating to harvest them, so there must be some level of DNA-encoding in a boy's system that desires construction and rebuilding.

I don't know how many phases of construction those mattresses went through, but I know that by the time I walked in, they had become the Alamo. Not a concert hall or a restaurant or a country lane flower shop, but a battlefield. The immediate and pressing desire was to build some sort of fortress to engage in warfare.

Fighting for Texas freedom that night was the complete assortment of guys. Davy Crockett was being played by a Jock (naturally). Jim Bowie was a Knucklehead. There were even a few Philosophers manning the battlements while commenting on the futility of war. The Gangster was shouting advice on Cheetoh-stabbing from the sidelines, and the Melting Pots were waging fearsome pillow combat.

The more subdued guys just sat there with goofy grins on their faces. Moody Musician was strumming on a guitar while his sidekick fired the thurting cannon, providing the modern day equivalent of a Texas Revolution fife and drum duet.

Each in their own way, all of the boys were linked by the

common desire to win the fight. Regardless of their makeup, as soon as the war drums sounded, it was *on*. With each pillow swung and plastic pellet fired, everything depended on being victorious.

It had begun as all wars throughout mankind's history had begun: One man had built up his mattresses, stock-piled the entire supply of Doritos, and defied all others in the room to "come and get them."

Battle lines had been drawn.

Countenances were set.

All would give some, and some would give all.

Those who wanted to see Doritos live in freedom could not stand by and do nothing.

Red-blooded young men from all walks of life heard the call of duty that evening. They put down their footballs, their guitars, and their lighters (that would be the Knuckleheads) and banded together for one last desperate struggle with a few good men.

Was it funny? Of course. But before you shrug it off as just boys being boys, let me emphasize once and for all time that they simply can't help themselves. If there is any possibility of conflict, boys will find a way to create it.

One of the most positive trends in recent men's literature is the emphasis on the way man was created. My father is a pastor, and it was through watching him that I first understood Christians could be manly, but I always figured he was just the rebel motorcycle gang leader of pastors.

For millions of men, though, no longer is the Bible just a collection of rules that we have to memorize in order to make our wives stop nagging us. God isn't only concerned with mercy and grace, but danger and adventure as well.

So it is not my intent to rehash a lot of that material. It's been done before. Just remember their desire for conflict is natural, ever present, and very necessary. The Jock sees his entire world through the lens of conflict because competition is what pleases him most. He is looking for a challenger to step forward and show, through word or deed, that he's hungry for a whuppin.' Jock will scan the sidelines of the opposing team for a cocky grin or an arrogant set of eyes that will tip him off to his challenger. Observing what that guy does on the field will provide him with the motivation to perform above his ability.

At any time when hanging out with his buddies, this young man will start a competition. If there happens to be a football nearby, then it's football. Should there not be a ball, the competition might take the form of a wrestling match or foot race.

I've noticed that of all the things that drive this kid crazy, being second place to someone is the worst. Particularly the Alpha Male. Sure, that would probably describe men across the board, but the difference is that Alpha Male gets most of his identity by being on top. I've seen teenagers old enough to be drafted fume for days after losing a basketball game on a retreat. In his world, nothing is worse than the other guy being better. If the other guy does better, that means he will get the praise, adulation, and girls.

The Philosopher will drum up conflict by saying and doing controversial things. He might dye his hair a dramatic color or wear a t-shirt specifically designed to anger mothers.

When I was in high school, there was a guy who showed up at school during Halloween dressed as a pregnant nun. Yes, you read that correctly. The predictable uproar ensued.

Anything that creates attention is worth pursuing for the Philosopher. He loves to be the guy in government class who will defend communism as a good idea gone bad simply because he loves the reaction it generates.

If he's scowling that means he is happy. If he is smiling that means he's unhappy. It's called having "ironic moods." He loves the exact opposite of what everyone else is doing.

I really enjoy these guys because I have a little bit of the Philosopher in me. I liked to say and believe things that defied all conventions simply because I didn't want to be part of the "crowd."

Before maturity sets in, this is a fun-filled fantasy land where *your* brain is the only brain that has ever been so powerful. The old saying is that the older you get the more you realize how dumb you actually are, and this is most true of the Philosopher. In order to create tension among people, the Philosopher will say something unpleasant and then retreat to watch events unfold.

Before I come across as sounding too light-hearted, let me put it in the record that I am aware of the genuine troubles some of these kids have. They aren't all troubled, but some of them are. All the teens I have ever been around have some level of the Philosopher in them because it is a heartfelt reaction to crummy situations in life.

The Moody Musician is primarily concerned with venting his frustrations to the world in much the same way as the Philosopher. If he just wants to rock because of the girls, then he might not be as tortured as he pretends. The conflict he loves is the day to day drama of relationships. For example, I'll watch the musician go through several different changes in the course of 15 minutes of hanging out with him. There's the laid back jokester. Not far behind comes the mildly annoyed know-it-all. Finally, as soon as someone says something that crosses the line, whining, anger, and pouting.

I've noticed that simple little dilemmas like not being able to afford a new pair of shoes this week can somehow manifest into a song about horrifying poverty and uncaring capitalists. A recent breakup with a girlfriend is sufficient life experience to declare all girls to be tramps.

Of course, there's also genuine talent. I've stood in awe of young guys who can flat out play the guitar. One of the best ways to help them think about deeper issues is pointing out that the ability to perform music is a gift from the Lord, and that simply by doing it you are worshipping. It might be misdirected worship, but it is worship nonetheless.

The Gangster loves conflict most of all because it gives him a chance to prove that he's The Man. Everyone growing up knew about The Man. The Man was the ruler of the elementary playground and never relinquished his throne the entire way through high school.

I remember clearly who The Man at my elementary school was. I'll call him Dominic, since that name sounds like "dominance." Dominic was The Man. You didn't question him, you didn't fight him, you did what you were told, and that was that.

If you wanted to play wall ball or foursquare at recess that day, you needed to clear it through Dominic first. Not only out of fear of physical punishment, but because The Man brought with him the girls. The girls were only going to be impressed with your foursquare abilities if they were actually present to watch you. Dominic ensured they were.

Dominic had his group of henchmen that he rolled with. If he was the Alpha Male, they were the young bucks vying for a spot in the herd. Thankfully, Dominic was a pretty laid back and friendly guy. As long as things were going smoothly, Dominic was easy to be around. If an individual questioned The Plan, the conversation went something like this:

Dominic's Henchman: "Hey, you, come here. Billy said that he heard from someone who told someone who said that you said that he said that we were playing foursquare today."

Geeky New Kid from Texas: "Um … well … yea, I thought … "

Henchman: "Clearly, you don't understand how things work around here. Dominic said we were playing wall ball today. You like girls, right?"

Geeky New Kid from Texas: "Well, yea."

Henchmen: "Okay then, if you want the girls to like you, and you want to be friends with us, then you need to do what we're all doing. And we do what Dominic does, capeesh?"

Geeky New Kid from Texas: "Um … okay, it's just that I … okay."

Alright, maybe I spiced it up with some mafia lingo, but you get the idea. You'll hear more about that geeky kid from Texas later.

The Gangster wants to be the authority over everyone. He'll create conflict and use the opportunity to reestablish order according to his own rules.

The Knucklehead is, obviously, a deep lover of conflict.

It's why he's called the Knucklehead. There isn't a thing he won't break in order to cause mayhem. Physical assault is a major part of this. He'll be in constant motion, trying to punch you on your arm or throw a ball at you. If a group of Knuckleheads are together, then they will be tossing handfuls of gravel at each other before too long.

The best part about Knuckleheads is that they rarely get their feelings hurt. Sure, it can happen, but I have noticed that even the most vicious taunting tends to be water off a duck's back.

For example, let's say that a fight breaks out among Knuckleheads who are traveling in a herd. Someone threw that last handful of gravel too hard, and now there's blood oozing down a forehead. The wounded party then lashes out with a savage left hook and the fight is on.

It lasts about two minutes and then ends up on the ground with each boy head-locking the other. Then someone in the group will shout something really funny and everyone starts cracking up. The two gladiators burst out in fits of laughter and release their headlocks.

The peace treaty is confirmed with something like this:

"Dude, sorry I threw those rocks at your head."

"Sorry I punched you."

"Cool."

"Cool."

I'm not making it up. Within five minutes of a fight to the death, the Knuckleheads are running around breaking things as happily as before.

When I'm up front on a Wednesday night doing my best to make spiritual concepts interesting, I like to look around at the stereotypes plainly visible:

In one corner of the room are some girls who think that by holding their cell phones down low I can't see them text messaging their friends. Nearby is what the youth staff calls "Lovers Lane," where each new couple formed that week will try and sit near one another. We tell them no physical touching while they're in the youth room, so it's quite funny watching them gaze like star-crossed lovers who are cruelly forced apart. The Gangsters chill in the back row and occasionally shoot me a disinterested look. The Moody Musicians are drumming their fingers on chairs, venting the constant rhythm in their heads. The Jock is doing his best to figure out a way to bounce a ball without me noticing. The Philosophers are listening attentively so they can catch me in some sort of contradiction and then point it out loudly to the group.

And then there are the Melting Pots. These guys make up the majority of the group. Each row of chairs is dominated by the Alpha Male of a category and all of his Melting Pot sidekicks. The first row is the chief Knucklehead and all his Melting Pot understudies. The second row is the Moody Musician leader, and so on.

Melting Pots are interesting because they will hopscotch from row to row. A kid that I was certain would become a Moody Musician suddenly laughs in the front row with the Knuckleheads. The conflict they feel is which row suits them the best.

If they sit in the first row with the Knuckleheads, they'll

be trying to come up with obnoxious things to do in order to impress the Alpha Male. If they plop down next to the Philosophers, they will live in a constant state of anguish trying to be ironic and critical.

The Melting Pot is the closest thing to the "normal kid" that you hear people talking about. If you have read all of these descriptions and can't decide which category best fits your teenager, chances are he's a Melting Pot.

RESPECT

At the age of ten I experienced my first desire for respect. At least the first one I can remember. I heard once that when I was a baby I tried to beat up other kids in the nursery. My grandmother informs me that my father did the same when he was a baby in the nursery. Maybe it's genetic.

My family moved to South Dakota all the way from Texas when my father felt called to pastor a church there. We had roots deep in the Lone Star State, so my mom wasn't thrilled with the prospect of moving where it's too cold for snow. Calling it snow would be too generous. It's more like "ice-chunking." South Dakota is a great place, but I can do without the ice-chunking. In the Great Far North (anywhere north of Amarillo to a Texan), they have these things called "seasons." The weather actually changes depending on the time of year. In Texas we have two seasons: hot and death. Mom is a proud Texan.

The drive north was made interesting by the arrival of a Canadian blizzard that buried us in Concordia, Kansas. For three days we waited out the snow, wondering why we'd left every friend and family member in our lives behind to live in a frozen wasteland (no offense, Concordia; you guys were terrific).

After arriving in Rapid City, my parents set about enrolling me in the local elementary school. Moving to a new town at the age of 10 is awkward enough, but I was also saddled with a Texas twang accent and a head three sizes too big for my body. Let me not forget to mention my giant red glasses, which made me look like Waldo from the children's books.

The first week was painful, but I managed to make it through to Friday. I even had a couple of kids look at me once or twice, so I thought new friends would be made very soon. As I left the final class of the day, I noticed that a group of students had gathered by one of the frosty windows. I saw what they were looking at and suddenly felt like I'd been force-fed a plate of tofu. Someone had written "Cliff is a loser" with her finger on the foggy glass. To make things worse, the girl who did it was the cutest girl in school.

I tore my hideous glasses off and ran from the hallway. I didn't even realize she knew who I was, much less thought that I was a loser. You know how there are events in your life that you're convinced at the time will haunt your dreams forever? That was one of them. I still have recurring nightmares of this event, but my wife assures me that *she* doesn't think I'm a loser. Whew.

The next encounter with respect happened on my very first youth group retreat. Seventh grade had just begun that fall, and it was a whole new world of thrilling opportunities. Okay, I made that up. Actually the first year of middle school was the most miserable that I can recall.

There was a mass sorting into different personality categories within the first week of September. Suddenly everyone was discovering how much freedom there was after elementary school, and girls were no longer considered to be disease-infested freaks. As we all broke off into our identities (Philosophers, Jocks, etc.), the goal was clear: earn respect.

October rolled around, and the youth group left on a retreat to Colorado. It was my first experience with the Big Kids who always played the loud music down the hall of the church. We crammed everyone into vans and hit the highway. Youth trip vans, like nurseries before them, are fascinating sociology experiments because you get to observe teenagers in their natural habitat. The difference is that they resemble nuclear waste dumps rather than natural habitats, and the smell would probably slaughter any cute little forest creature that innocently hopped into them.

The major purpose of retreats, as I was about to find out, isn't the spiritual renewal. That's the goal of the leaders. In the eyes of the students, retreats are three entire days away from your parents to make your move on that cute girl at school who comes to Wednesday night services. Sure, they can be great spiritual experiences, but teenagers are teenagers.

We always broke it down into three phases. The first phase was the van ride to retreat, the farther away the better. Boys all jockeyed for positioning in the van with the girls, and as the miles droned by, you sat in your seat scheming how best to say the funniest remark or draw the most attention to yourself.

If that girl didn't know you existed before the ride, she was bound to know it by the time you got done impressing her with your bodily functions or witty jokes. The louder you spoke in the vans the more likely she was to discover your existence. This is where the first sorting of mice and men took place, because those of us in the 7th grade didn't have our masculine voice tones yet. All of my shouts for attention sounded like a rubber ducky squeaking in the bathtub.

Phase two began when you actually arrived at the retreat. The whole weekend, in between sessions and meals, you worked up the nerve to actually *talk* to her. This is a monumentally difficult task. Your buddies are coaching you as you walk to the breakfast hall after the first night and when you get inside, you see all the girls sitting around a large table. Fear hits you. It's casual conversation at first with everyone sharing the funny stories from the night before. Pillow fights, Mountain Dew rockets, various other shenanigans. You try and find a way to be the funniest one at the table and steal glances at the girl to see if she is watching you.

If you are being politely engaged, that means she thinks you're a loser and is politely engaging you. Or, worse, it might be your friend she's interested in and she's only using you to get to him. You also learn on this retreat just how tangled a web that girls can weave when it comes to relationships.

If you are being completely ignored, then you know you have a shot, because she might be trying to act hard-to-get. The first thing to watch for is whether her friends are looking at you a lot, because she's going to rely on their reports when they all get back to the dorm rooms.

At some point during the weekend, sandwiched between the sessions, is an opportunity to display your courage and masculinity. It's usually a dodge ball match or an inflatable jousting tournament. Regardless, the goal is to defeat all the other boys at whatever it is. This will hopefully woo her enough to reward you with a smile and a blush.

If you are the victor and beat the other guys, then you

get to reap the rewards. If you don't, there's an agonizingly long period of time before the next meal where you have no opportunities to impress her again. She's going to be hanging out with the *winner*, see, and while you may be invited along, you're not the center of attention—the winner is. Despair gnaws away at the boy who never wins. He's never good enough, never strong enough, never fast enough, never funny enough, never, never, never...

Phase three of the retreat was the van ride home. This was where I knew I would finally have my shot. It seemed like all of the other guys on this particular retreat were Alpha Males. I was a scrawny, quiet, and unknown weakling, but I loved to laugh, and by some miracle I was able to gain the attention of my peers.

Joke after joke kept coming into my head, and I was the star of the van ride home. It seemed like I could do no wrong. All of the best looking girls were poking my shoulder and laughing and talking about how funny I was. The other guys were laughing at me, a little jealous of my attention but still supportive. I had turned a whole new leaf. No longer would I be the *ordinary* guy.

Monday morning, when we returned back to school, none of those kids even gave me the time of day. They gave me a few nodded greetings and some obligatory glances, but for the most part, my social status returned to what it was before. I bumbled awkwardly through the lunch line, bumbled awkwardly to my locker, and bumbled awkwardly through math class. (That never changed all the way through college.) Whatever respect I gained had been fleeting. Most people will agree that middle school is among the cruelest of life's phases. If you don't think so, then you were one of the few who didn't bumble awkwardly.

For respect, a man will do anything.

Jocks want admiration from the fans, fear from the opponents, and attention from the girls. Philosophers want people to envy how smart they are. They take their activities very seriously because they want to be thought of seriously. They want to be the guy everyone turns to for the answer to a question. Moody Musicians desperately want to "make it." They're completely devoted to their craft and believe that somehow, if the song is just right, people will stand in awe of them.

Gangsters demand that everyone be reminded of how *they* are in control. Knucklehead wants to be remembered through history as the guy who did something so stupid, so hilarious, and so death-defying that the memory of it will live on forever in the songs of their people.

The Melting Pot? He doesn't care where it comes from—he just wants respect. He wants to be *someone*. He wants people to notice him for *something*. Nothing is worse than being the nice kid you forget about immediately after meeting him.

This is precisely why video games have become so popular. The phenomenal rise of the industry is measured in the billions of dollars. The gaming companies now make the same amount of money as all of Hollywood, and the numbers continue to grow.

You see, in a virtual world a boy can be *exceptional*. By day he is a geeky middle school boy with scrawny shoulders, but by night he is Zyzor the Barbarian Warlord, conqueror of worlds. He wins every fight and never fails in whatever he tries. His friends respect him if he has the highest score in a video game, because now gaming is done over the internet and the entire world can see his achievements. They stand amazed at him as he blasts his way through thousands of enemies. Gym class may be humiliating because he can't climb the rope, but it doesn't bother him. He knows that when he gets home all the virtual girls in the video game will admire him.

Many never outgrow it. It's why grown men will waste their entire adult lives living a virtual life, because it fills the void in their heart created by all the failure and rejection. It's a risk-free endeavor to be a tough guy in virtual reality because you can plunder, pillage, and sleep with whoever you want without any real world consequences.

Video games don't have to be the enemy; quite the contrary, I have found them to be enormously useful in connecting with young men. We'll look at that later. For now, understand that the desire for respect can drive a young man to do anything, including waste his life away in front of a computer screen fighting imaginary battles and ignoring real ones.

A boy's desire for respect is important to understand because it corresponds to why he may not want to come to church. If he enters a church building and is only told what *not* to do and how to act, he perceives that people in the building don't respect him. Many who read that will probably say, "He's just a kid, Cliff, and being told what to do is a part of life." Hey, you're talking to an Army officer. I agree completely. The difference is in *how* we tell them what to do.

For instance, I am a pretty well-read person. Books are

a major love of mine. If I were to follow you around and demand that you become interested in Tolstoy's *War and Peace*, you would most likely wish I wasn't doing that. Unless you are a fellow readaholic I can't force you to want to read 19th century Russian literature. Likewise, if you are a lover of mathematics, not even the threat of a blow to my head with a spiked club would make me the least bit curious about your world. Seriously, not even then. And I don't want to hear about how wonderful and easy math is. Even the friendly and sacrificial teachers gave up on me, rightfully so.

However, if the two of us decided that we were going to make a choice to find something interesting about each other's interests, then it would clearly be a better starting point in building a relationship. We may never fall in love with the other's hobbies ourselves, but we would be able to see the passion each of us had for them. If you demonstrate a genuine willingness to hear about 19th century Russian literature, I'll swallow the pain and listen to you about math. To affirm a boy for who he is and what his interests are, regardless of how wacky they seem, is to make the first step in showing the kid that Jesus can be an enjoyable person to get to know.

Shaunti Feldhahn did some intriguing research into the inner thoughts of men for her book *For Women Only*. She cited surveys conducted by a professional polling group that indicated a truth which nearly all men have in common: a desperate, all-encompassing need for respect. In one such survey, 74% of men said they would rather be alone and unloved in the world than be disrespected by people.

It does not require scholarly research to understand that

respect is the ruthless taskmaster which drives men forward. Wives, this explains why he never asks for directions. It has nothing to do with directions and everything to do with the perceived lack of respect he will get from the gas station attendant he is forced to ask directions from.

If you're a man reading this, you know what I'm talking about. We *need* respect, even if we won't tell the people at church or in the office for fear of looking arrogant. This isn't to say that respect is the goal of our lives; rather, it is affirmation of who we are as men. Jesus grew in the stature and favor of men, as it says in Luke 2:52. He didn't need to go looking for it. He provided the perfect example of living to those around Him, and a natural byproduct of that was respect.

Boys *must* feel like they are going to be respected if they are going to get anything out of church. They need to know that their opinion is valuable, even if it's stupid. Don't worry, parents: the older they get, the smarter you will appear to them.

All guys share a few key traits in common. Recognizing these traits is necessary to understanding how we can better communicate the message of Christ to teenage boys. All boys have the desire to create chaos and rebuild it again, the desire to engage in conflict, and the desire for respect.

(They all lose their socks a lot, too.)

TRUE FOR ME,
BUT NOT FOR THEE

We have a nice church facility, but the roof leaks whenever it rains, and it always seems to leak directly over a computer. It makes no difference where we move them because the leaks are everywhere at once. We've fixed them multiple times, and yet they leak. Just when we think the leaks have been stopped, they reignite elsewhere across the building. Usually right above a computer that was moved to avoid the leaks.

The original intent of the place was to bring in lots of people to spend lots of cash. It's a former outlet mall and sits squarely in the part of town that is the last place you'd think to put a church building. There are factory warehouses surrounding the property and the neighborhood nearby isn't exactly the upper crust of San Antonio society.

As you walk up to the front doors, you're smacked in the face by a sign with one word: "Jesus."

There's no catchy marketing slogan, no glamorous publications about building your life one block at a time. Ten Step Solution Guy would probably look down his nose at it. There's just the phrase "Jesus." printed over the doorway. And let me not forget to mention that the period is on the sign as well. Jesus Period.

Crossing over the threshold, you notice the forty-foot wide hallways and window-front rooms. Where merchants used to sell goods, people are now meeting for Sunday school. The wide hallways were designed to hold folks hustling and bustling from one store to the next in order to buy some tennis shoes, toys, and short-lived happiness.

There are potholes in the parking lot you could go spelunking in and rumor has it the baptistery structure might collapse into the netherworld at any moment. Back in the day, a possum fell out of the ceiling. Another one ran across the stage *during the service*. I really wish I could have been there to see it.

Then there's the youth room. The youth section of any church in America probably needs to be decontaminated more often. I don't mean swept and vacuumed. I'm talking about full-on chemical biohazard decontamination. There's an odor in the carpet that can only be described as indescribable. The years of pizza, soda, sweat, and socks (I'm telling you, they're everywhere) have created a symphony of nastiness. All kidding aside, we keep it clean and well-maintained, but I don't think anyone with a straight face can tell you their youth room smells of roses and sunshine.

Okay so it doesn't look like a "church." But if you're looking for an example of people who want Jesus and not religion, it fits the bill. *Jesus* and not *religion*. Confusing those two drives young men away from church in ever increasing numbers. Boys who reach the age of eighteen are walking out the doors of the service and never coming back. George Barna, a Christian pollster, reports that only about 9 percent of all born-again adults have a thoroughly biblical worldview. This includes the beliefs that Satan is a real person, that there is any absolute truth in the world, and what is written in Scripture is true without any mixture of error. Scary stuff, right? Here's where it gets scarier: the people who come to church are no different. Neither are their children.

These aren't the rebel gothic kids that you may see hanging around the schoolyard. These are Bible-raised, Church-going teenagers. When we hear things like that, there can be a couple of reactions. The first is that young people aren't as spiritual as they used to be and simply need more Bible teaching. The other reaction could be that there are too many bad influences outside the home drawing them away.

I think there's an element of truth in both. A lack of Scriptural grounding is prevalent among young people, and there are a lot of influences that can be harmful. But, from what I have seen, pushing "church" into a kid can foster resentment and bitterness. Their understanding of Jesus becomes distorted into yet another self-help strategy that parents are forcing on them. There's no call to action that speaks to a boy's heart, no bigger story that ignites the fire of imagination. Authentic pursuit of Jesus has been replaced by a list of what not to do. Nowhere is there room for life.

Before I get too far into that, it's important to first understand how we have come to this point. The modern world is very different than it was for even the previous generation, and the fast rise of technology has brought with it a huge variety of worldviews that young people are exposed to.

There's been much written, deservedly so, about the generation that came out of World War II, called the "Greatest Generation." It was personified by hard work and dedication to a greater cause. Patriotism was understood as being inherent among all Americans. There were very clear rights and wrongs in society. It was right to fight off the Nazis, right to respect the leaders of the government, and right to honor your mother and father. Churches contained a lot of orderly family units. Preachers were revered as leaders in the community.

When something was determined to be morally wrong, there was a general consensus among the population to avoid it. There were exceptions, obviously, but by and large people understood there was a higher moral law that we should all live under.

Then came the Baby Boom generation. My parents are baby Boomers, and I have endlessly teased them about it. Many of you reading this are Baby Boomers. It was marked by a rebellion against all authority of any kind. Whatever institutions were in place to oppress you, you were to toss them off and live free. (Sometimes that tossing included your clothing, and I'm really glad I wasn't around for that.)

There were many great movements towards justice and equality, so we can't be too hard on Baby Boomers. Civil rights became a major issue, and it was good for society to help some churches recognize that all men really were created equal, and that there shouldn't be a division among people based upon race or ethnicity. Cultural differences will always prevent complete spiritual harmony here on earth, but we need not hate each other.

Another positive movement out of this time was an increased freedom in worship style. Thunderous preaching and robed choirs were the previously accepted standard for many in the church culture. When long-haired hippies with guitars started strumming songs about Jesus there were cries of heresy and danger from some corners.

Thankfully, others saw that God does not limit Himself to choir music, and a lot of young preachers started getting back to the basics of the Message. These guys did the same exact thing that a man named Martin Luther did in the 1500's: they cracked open the Bible, saw a bunch of stuff the church was doing and forcing onto people that wasn't written in Scripture, and decided there needed to be room for the real Jesus in the worship service once again.

To clarify, I am not contending that God wasn't moving in the traditional services. He is powerful and present wherever His people call for Him. What I am suggesting is that as times began to change, the old methods weren't always working with younger people, and a modern reformation took place.

This leads us to young people today; my generation, and the generation of current teenagers: the Millenials.

We grew up learning computer skills from early on in elementary school. Classes were devoted to teaching us the language of technology, exactly the same as Spanish or German class. We became fluent in word-processing and internet usage.

I tried teaching my mother four hundred times about how to use the internet. She's one of the smartest people I know and her advice on life is invaluable to me, but she doesn't know a single thing about how to operate what she calls "those internet thingys." She can check her email, but if I try and send her an attachment she gets frightened and deletes it. If you don't know what I mean by "attachment" you belong in the same category as mom.

My father is much worse. Again, the usual bit about how smart and wise he is, but he couldn't be more clueless about information technology. I've given up teaching him how to operate a computer and told him to be content with letting other people handle things like his church's website. This is the same man who thought the CD player in his car was a slot that held your mail.

Some of you in that generation are extremely computer savvy but I promise you that you're in the minority. The rest of your generation has been left behind, so let me take this opportunity to encourage you to help your peers. The Internet is not a passing fad, as my mother once called it. It's here to stay. Why not embrace it?

At some point during the twentieth century, and scholars debate exactly when, something called "postmodernism" began to emerge. I've read a lot about what this word actually means, and the best definition I have found is that it's the natural result of total rebellion.

The religions of the East, such as Hinduism, began to creep into America. Typical of Eastern thought is the concept that there are many versions of truth. This is really pretty funny because if you say there are many versions of truth, how do you know that's a true statement? Around and around we go. As the OSG Alexander Hamilton once put it, "A man who stands for nothing will fall for anything."(OSG means Old Smart Guy).

If the Greatest Generation stood for good versus evil, and the Baby Boomers stood for rebellion against that, then the Millennials stand for nothing. The problem is not their desire to rebel against authority; it's that they have no desire to *care* about anything.

Living in this mindset leads one to conclude that truth does not really exist. At least not truth that we all have to obey and adhere to. Heck, what's true for you is great as long as you don't impose that truth on others. The *worst* thing someone can do in our culture is to offend somebody, even if it means warning them to get out of the way of a speeding bus:

"Hey, lady, get out of the way of that bus!"

"How *dare* you call me 'lady!' I am not some piece of meat that you can___ "

Wam!

Since truth doesn't matter to anyone, this has a devastating effect on morals. There's no reason to call anything "right" or "wrong" unless you can provide a standard for those words. To label something "wrong" means that there is a perfect measure of "right" you are comparing it to.

For example, most everyone will agree that feeding starving orphans in Africa is a good thing to do, even those who are complete atheists. One of the obnoxious questions I like to ask our kids is, "Why is feeding an orphan a good thing to do?" The blank stares they give me are classic. Of course it's good, why wouldn't it be? The problem is that if you don't believe in any form of absolute truth, then you have to conclude there is no objective standard of morality to judge things against. If you claim to be an atheist and don't believe in a morally perfect deity who makes the rules, then you lose the right to say anything I do is right or wrong.

These are all examples of the arguments that C.S. Lewis, Francis Schaeffer, G.K. Chesterton, and a bunch of other OSG's made. As wars raged and millions were slaughtered throughout the twentieth century, they were seeing the inevitable result of mankind living without God.

Another person who saw it was a man named Friedrich Nietzsche. He was the German philosopher most admired by Hitler, who, in turn, gave copies of his books to Stalin and Mussolini. In a famous book called *The Gay Science*, Nietzsche came to his conclusion that God was dead and man had killed Him. What he meant was that mankind had finally progressed to the understanding that there was no longer a God to rely on.

The interesting part of this, however, is that instead of jubilation Nietzsche was filled with sorrow. He understood the consequences of his idea that there was no God. No longer could things be considered right or wrong because if we are all just chance accidents of biology, then we should have no higher moral codes than animals do.

So when Hitler killed his millions, and Stalin and Mao killed their tens of millions, we were seeing the inevitable results of removing God and the annoying moral laws He brings with Him. The strong survive, and if you were weak then you were in the way of progress and needed to be eliminated.

The modern world is considered to be the time between

the Enlightenment and the turn of the 20th century. From 1900 until the present, we are seeing the *post*modern world. Greatest Generation and Baby Boom folks experienced the birth pains of it, and Millenials are living it in full.

Young people, through the medium of the internet and television, are smacked with so many different worldviews that they no longer care what to believe. The response is to just tune out. Here's postmodernism in a nutshell: "There is no moral that you should have except the moral of having no morals. If it makes you happy, do it, but don't offend me. If you worship God, that's fine, but don't project that onto me. We are all looking for the same God after all, aren't we?"

I could bore everyone some more about postmodernism, but I won't. Just remember that it is the culprit for a lot of what you see. It explains teen behavior the best. I'm not try-ing to contend that teenagers sit around and think about this stuff, but they *are* the products of postmodern culture.

Whenever they sit in a classroom and listen to a nice motivational speaker named Chester tell them how impor-tant their self-esteem is and how being a judgmental reli-gious person is harmful, you can be certain that postmodern-ism is the shadowy puppet master.

So what about the church attendance crisis?

In reaction to the turmoil brought about by this cultural shift, I have noticed that many young men associate churches with mean people who make a lot of rules. Their parents drag them to church, they hear a lot of do's and don'ts, and their entire perception of God is that He is some old man with a long beard sitting on a throne in the clouds handing out commandments in order to make life as boring as possible.

This may be the view of God given by the culture and it may be the message sent out from some churches, but it is not the Jesus of the Scriptures. He was loving, passionate, dedicated, fierce, and *likeable*.

One bright summer day I was talking to some teen guys about their perception of God. They were Melting Pots, so their opinions are pretty consistent with other teens. They spent a great deal of time explaining to me how they couldn't figure out why mom and dad were always on their case about Jesus. One of them even said that he didn't understand why it was such a big deal to his folks to make him listen to all of the church stuff. Why couldn't they just do it themselves and be happy and let him do his own thing? (Thanks again, postmodernism.)

One of the other interesting parts of our conversation was when one of them mentioned that he had never heard from God, not once, not ever.

"What makes you say that?" I asked him.

"Well, I see all these people running around and saying how God told them this and God told them that. It seems like God is even telling people whether they should buy Pepsi or Coke and all the while I've never heard from Him in my life."

I pondered that a moment, then replied, "What's your view of Jesus?"

"He's cool. I just don't understand, you know, I can't hear Him telling me things like He seems to tell other people things. It's really intimidating. My parents just think I'm not listening to Him enough, but how can I listen when I don't hear anything?"

I talked with him a little about how the Holy Spirit is the

presence of Jesus inside us and I think he seemed to understand the need to ask for Him. But the root of his anguish was pretty evident: he felt intimidated by other Christians who were trying to demand that he experience God in one particular way, the way that *they* experience Him. Another young man once complained to me that he can't stand being forced to go out of the country on mission trips. He appreciates the work of those who do but there is simply no desire in him to leave the city and go with them.

This isn't the place to get involved in lengthy discussions about the work of the Holy Spirit, but I do want to suggest that there's no single way to experience Him. Paul wrote, "And He gave some as apostles, and some as prophets, and some as evangelists, and some as pastors and teachers" (Ephesians 4:11).

He was referring to those who have the work of equipping the saints, but from that verse we can see that we each have different gifts from God. We're not all required to be every category at once. This misunderstanding has somehow crept into the minds of church teenagers and has put a pressure on them that is hard to overstate.

In recent years it would seem that the church has removed biblical education from spiritual impartation. That's a fancy way of saying that we care more about the amount of material stuffed into one brain than the day-to-day application of that material. The church teaches the children Bible stories, makes the teenagers memorize all sixteen chapters of Romans, and then assumes it has done its job in discipleship. Those same teenagers are then expected to function as fully mature believers.

I've visited churches where they parade Miracle Guy out on the stage and succeed in scaring the daylights out of everyone in the service. Miracle Guy is the dude that used to drink every bottle of booze in sight and sleep with every woman in town until he finally got saved. Now he never, *ever* struggles with sin or temptation, and it's all because he memorized 371 verses.

Extreme? Perhaps. But I think such stories are more prevalent than we realize. It's stressful to think that everyone has it figured out but you. The type of spiritual arrogance that motivates someone like Miracle Guy leads to complete disillusionment towards church, because the people watching it who came to know Christ and still struggle with their sin believe they aren't Christians. Miracle Guy is telling a lie when he says he doesn't struggle anymore. We gotta call him on it. Lives are transformed mightily by the saving grace of Christ, but becoming a Christian does not automatically render you sinless. We will continue to sin until the day of Christ's return; the difference is that we are forgiven of that sin and *have the desire* to walk in righteousness.

The idea that just teaching the Bible is the only acceptable way to tell teenagers about Jesus isn't working. Simple Scripture memorization, while great for hiding God's word away in our minds, doesn't automatically hide it away in our hearts. We have to chew it and meditate on it, something that you can't force on people.

I will share my faith when the opportunity arises and develop relationships with people in the hopes that they come to know the real Jesus, but I don't have the *gift* of evangelism. I work with people who do and the Lord can powerfully move through those men and women in order to save the lost. It also humbles me into remembering that I don't have the same gift and shouldn't live under the slavery and arrogance of thinking that I do. I don't have any right to tell God what my gifts should be.

I remember very clearly the day I discovered I was not going to be Billy Graham's successor. It was a hot summer in downtown Denver, Colorado and we were on a youth mission trip to help rebuild some churches in the inner city. It was fantastic work, hammering away at nails and goofing around with the hacksaws. The heart of the organization we were with was to show Christ's love to people by performing service acts.

I loved doing the actual work, but the experience of walking the street and passing out gospel tracts was terrible for me. This isn't a commentary on the merits of gospel tracts, I've seen God use them and we give them out at events. It's just that I don't have the desire or ability to grab every person I see and blurt out my testimony with a piece of paper. It's difficult to defend with Scripture that we all *need* to be passing gospel tracts out. By the same token, it's also difficult to say that *no one* should be passing them out. Neither is correct. We ought to show the young men in our congregations that we encourage each other's particular gifting and not always assume others have those giftings.

For a long time I lived under the slavery of assuming that I was failing God because I didn't want to be a street evangelist. I believed that I wasn't doing enough for the Kingdom and that Jesus was going to stand at the Judgment and point his finger at me and demand how many souls I saved with my time on earth. It was bondage, and it was false theology. You and I don't save *anyone's* soul. Christ handles all that. We're the instruments He chooses to use in order to spread the message about Himself. We're certainly responsible to be obedient to Him with our calling and gifts, but the actual work of salvation is not done by you and I.

Parents might not have explicitly given their kids that belief, and it may not have been preached outright at church, but it's an unspoken assumption when around "religious" people. Boys are experiencing the stress of it, I see it every week.

The warning order is loud and clear: Boys don't care about spiritual matters. The common traits of bringing order out of chaos, desiring conflict, and craving respect have been largely ignored by the Christian community. So how do we show them the real Jesus? Operation Orders to follow.

PART ★ TWO

IT'S OKAY TO
LAUGH IN CHURCH

Situation:

> Teenage boys believe that knowing Jesus means you have to be serious and boring all the time.

Mission:

> Help them understand that He is the creator of laughter.

Execution:

★ INCLUDE LAUGHTER IN WORSHIP

Somewhere back yonder (a little Southern lingo for you) it became improper to laugh when it came to Church Time. Oh sure, the youth were permitted their little fun activities and it was all fine and good to bust a gut at the next pot-luck dinner, but when church time started, all frivolity had to cease. Who came up with that? I'd love to know.

Thumbing through the Scriptures, I don't see anywhere that God bans laughter from His worship service. Here's the logic: if all good things come from God, and laughter is a good thing, then technically speaking, you can have a laughter worship service to praise Him.

Before someone tosses this thing down in disgust, hear me out. One of the most successful ways to get the attention of teenagers is doing something spectacularly funny. This is most true of the Knuckleheads, who see it as their goal in life to waste nary a minute with something other than goofing off.

There are, obviously, boundaries to this. A time of fasting and prayer is not the best moment to try out your new Water-Squirting Rubber Chicken. But we can utterly destroy the prospects of a young man wanting to hear more about Jesus if we feel the need to cram every available minute of a service with nothing but Scripture study. I understand that most churches and Christians have no problem with any of that but there are many who do. It's why a lot of their kids run crazy once they hit college—fun is a foreign concept to them.

Our Wednesday night services are usually around two hours long. Out of those two hours, an hour and a half is spent eating, laughing, talking, and playing. The last half hour is when we teach the kids a lesson. Sometimes it's a specific passage out of the Bible and sometimes it isn't.

There is always a section of God's Word that we try to communicate, but one thing I know for sure: If I try and walk verse by verse through the book of Ephesians on a Wednesday night when all manner of street kids are hanging out in there, they would (1) fall right asleep, or (2) start "thurting" me.

I've wrestled with the Lord many times over why it seems like none of our kids take anything seriously. I've poured hours into lessons only to be forced into shouting over the noise. The thought that we might be ignoring the Holy Spirit kept sneaking into the minds of our stalwart youth staff. Then talking to a buddy one day, another youth leader friend named Lee, I realized something crucial. Lee asked me whether I remembered anything at all that I learned in youth group growing up.

That struck me as an odd question. Sure I learned stuff! I remember the youth pastor Todd always saying ... well, I recall that we once talked about ... and then I realized that I didn't remember anything he taught us. I can recall certain subjects he was passionate about and occasional topics he covered, but specific words he communicated are lost to antiquity.

Well shoot, that's depressing, I thought to myself. These kids won't remember anything I taught them? That's when Lee said something I will never forget.

"You don't remember everything Todd ever told you, but you remember Todd."

That's the meat worth smoking (more Texas lingo). He was right; I don't remember many specific things that Todd taught us, except for the occasional prank that required astounding engineering abilities. But I *do* remember that Todd was one of the funniest people I had ever met, that I grew a lot in my relationship with Christ by seeing his unorthodox methods, and I remember doing it while laughing my head off.

Here's an example of how laughter communicates a concept: The boys who go on our retreats always seem to smell bad. We can pressure wash them all we want and yet the stench never leaves. It's like they apply Dead Rat cologne when they wake up each morning. In addition, the boys leave all their trash scattered on the floors of the cabins and tents and they do it no matter how many times I tell them to pick it up.

Along with all their socks.

One summer camp I finally had enough and suddenly

ordered all of them to cram into the bath house. With quizzical faces they crowded into showers and stalls.

"Okay, men," I shouted over the noise, "on the count of three we are going to start mooing like cows. If we're going to live like livestock, then we're going to act like livestock!"

The girls had a great time watching all the boys mooing in unison. You'd have thought I was a cowboy driving the herd to the Dodge City railways. The point was made and they thought it was funny. Now whenever I see trash scattered about, I threaten them with another round of mooing.

Laughter. It's powerful. Never underestimate the ability of humor to speak truth to a teenager. They won't remember me yelling at them, but they'll remember the mooing.

With your teen guy, it doesn't matter what category he is. The Jock, the Philosopher, the Moody Musician, the Gangster, the Knucklehead, and the Melting Pot love to see or hear something funny. If the Bible contains no humor, then somebody please explain to me why the Lord made a donkey start talking to Balaam. That's funny stuff.

Some say that keeping things serious is a matter of reverence for God, and I agree with them. I'm not advocating food fights during the Sunday sermon. It's just a matter of making fun a priority. We can't get horrified and offended by petty things like boys running down the hallways bonking each other with Nerf bats. Pull them aside and ask them to settle down? Perfectly fine. But they didn't commit murder so we need not act as if they did. Fun feeds life, and *life* should be the goal of church activities.

Some of the old movies made about the life of Jesus have given an absolutely horrendous depiction of who He actually was. The guy floating around in a perfectly white robe with blue eyes and an English accent is not the same Jesus who lived on earth. Do we honestly think the inventor of laughter never once told a joke on earth?

There have been parents who approached me with concerns about what they see going on in our youth room. Maybe they don't like the fact that we don't do more Scripture memorization, or they think there isn't enough praise and worship music in our service. We listen to any concerns a parent may have and try to share our heart, which is pretty simple: Teenagers need to associate Jesus with laughter and fun.

We'll speak hard truths to them. We don't shy away from the realities of heaven and hell. We want to beckon them to a deeper walk with Christ. But the opposite of laughter and life is crying and death, and there's enough of that going on in the world. Church fellowship ought to be a place to escape it and encourage those suffering through it.

My parents are frequently asked why my sister and I never felt the need to rebel as preacher's kids. PK's are scrutinized severely throughout their early years and many end up going crazy. I can't say I blame them. It's tough under the microscope.

I think what made the difference was the amount of laughter in my house. My mother stands alone as the funniest person I've ever known, bar none. No comedian who ever performed can crack me up like my mom getting into another pickle.

Whether it's falling into the dumpster behind my apartment, trying to make a bank deposit on Veterans Day when the bank is closed, or eating cereal while applying makeup in the car on the way to church, mom is the standard-bearer of laughter.

My dad is really funny as well, and the two of them together are hysterical. I was blessed to see that side of God all my days under their roof.

No matter how tough some of life's growing pains were, that house never went a day without laughter. For the rest of my life, I will associate Jesus with happiness and a good belly-aching laugh.

There's more to Him than comedy. He's the Righteous Judge. But please, don't let your son assume God just wants to ruin the fun of every party; that somehow if people are laughing in a room, and the Christian walks in, they have to suddenly shut up because they're afraid of offending him. Kids outside our church culture need to know that Jesus means life, freedom, and so much comedy that your brain hurts just thinking about it.

So if you're discouraged because your son only talks about the goofy stunts the youth pastor pulled in church or just mentions the food he ate when you ask him about Wednesday night services, don't panic. As long as someone who follows Jesus is influencing him, that's all he's going to remember anyway.

I don't remember everything my mom and dad taught me, but I remember their influence. I don't remember Todd's exact words, but I remember Todd. I remember his influence. Your son won't always remember the specifics of what you said to him. But he *will* remember your influence and the laughter that was or wasn't allowed, and when he thinks about God you can be sure that somewhere in the back of his mind he's thinking about you.

HANG OUT THEOLOGY

Situation:

> Many Christians believe that Jesus is only present when there are serious events like preaching, prayer, or fasting going on. Boys lose interest in church as a result.

Mission:

> Help boys realize that Christ can be found in times of fun.

Execution:

★ UNDERSTAND THAT CHRIST SPENT TIME HANGING OUT

Jesus, while he lived on earth, hung out with people. He really would. What was the deep theological meaning of this? He liked hanging out. The proof is that in the Gospels whenever he showed up at someone's house, another person usually started the conversation with Him. Matthew 9:9–13 is the story of Jesus calling Matthew the tax collector and then attending a banquet. He was "reclining" at the table when someone asked him a question, leading to a response.

Apparently, Jesus was just sitting and enjoying the company of His fellow guests. He knew that important subjects would eventually come up, but He didn't go out of His way to condemn people. He simply liked hanging out.

Obviously, hanging out wasn't the main point of what He was up to. There are plenty of times where the Gospels describe his commanding speeches calling the people to repentance. He drives out evildoers from the temple with a whip (one of my favorites). Then there are the conversations with the women, something *totally* unheard of in that time. No self-respecting man had anything to do with women in public.

Pretty much nothing Jesus did fit with any preconceived notions of who the people thought He would be. And I would be so bold as to suggest that "hanging out" was part of that. Pharisees followed Jesus around trying to catch him in a contradiction of the law so they could jump up and down and shout, "See! See! We told you he wasn't the guy! Ha!" Every time they thought they had Him, He would deftly elude them once more.

Why was he wasting time with all these sinners? *If this street rabbi with calloused hands is the King he says he is*, they must have wondered, *then why isn't he going to the parties thrown by the wealthy?* The answer is that he *did* go to those parties, such as the banquet mentioned above, and even then the Pharisees criticized Him.

In Matthew 11:19 Jesus makes plain his exasperation with religious hypocrites: "For John came neither eating nor drinking, and they say, 'He has a demon!' The Son of Man came eating and drinking, and they say, 'Behold, a gluttonous man and a drunkard, a friend of tax collectors and sinners!' Yet wisdom is vindicated by her deeds" (Matthew 11:18–19).

He hung out with everyone. Status in life didn't matter;

Jesus wanted the hungry hearts. He desires mercy, not sacrifices, according to Matthew 9:13. A person who doesn't know the Bible from the phone book, but knows he needs Jesus, is the person Christ comes near.

★ TEACH THEM THAT JESUS WANTS AUTHENTICITY.

There has been a lot of positive movement in churches recently in regards to getting back to the heart of Jesus, but one of the unfortunate results of this new wave of change is that some are motivated by rebellion. The desire to bring about reform can't be born out of a rebellious heart, and the belief has crept in that only the poor or those with a radically new worship service experience true spirituality.

Jesus lifted up the position of the poor and taught the people that they needed to be broken and humble before the Lord. In Matthew 5:17, He also said that He didn't come to abolish the law, but to fulfill it. The Holy Spirit can be just as present in a punk rock church as He might be in the fanciest cathedral in the city. Likewise, the punk rock church shouldn't feel the need to throw out every single tradition just because it's a tradition.

To a teenager, who has no interest whatsoever in church, this can be the final straw. Denominational bickering makes all churches look phony. Big spiritual words and long discussions about church constitutions won't help him understand the real Jesus. To reach the heart of a young man, we have to study less Systematic Theology and more Hang Out Theology.

"Hanging Out" is defined as sitting around, talking, laughing and coming up with fun things to do. In the midst of it there could be some serious conversation, but the goal of the hanging out is to develop a relationship. Let me illustrate it this way. Every once in a while a mother or father will bring their teenager into our youth room and ask what we can do to "fix" their child. I see the terrible concern on their faces because they're desperate to try anything. Self-help books haven't worked, daytime chit chat television didn't help, and they've tried everything else with the same result. Worse, they went to a church that promised quick-fixes and ten step solutions and left thinking something was wrong with them. Maybe the mom or dad has discovered the life-changing power of Christ and can't figure out why their child isn't on fire with passion like they are.

The answer we give is that there's absolutely nothing we can do to *fix* their kid. Only Jesus fixes people, and it's best not to pretend that we have anything to do with it. I do say this, however. We're committed to creating an environment for the kids to come and relax in. They feel comfortable walking through our doors. They eat our food. No one is following them around demanding that they do things. They just *hang out*. Once a guy feels like no one in there is trying to convert him or intimidate him with spiritual language, he can be real with himself and others. He can laugh, have a good time, and, eventually, he will allow the smallest peek into his heart.

One night I was sitting next to a Moody Musician/Jock combo who was trying to explain to me, over fish sticks and fries, why he was so frustrated with God. We were blasting space aliens in a game and I was finally holding my own. Out of nowhere (as usual) he started talking.

"I believe in God, dude. I'm just tired of my parents trying to get me to quote verses and all that sort of stuff. Mom can be creepy sometimes, all this stuff about anointing people and all that."

I replied, "So your problem isn't really with God, it's with your folks, right?"

"Yeah, I 'spose."

I told him about how his parents were doing their best and to cut them some slack, but you can hear once again how these guys misunderstand what knowing Christ is all about. It was a perfect example of Hang Out Theology. No more complicated than that. Taking the time to get to know a kid before bombarding him with questions of spirituality makes him feel comfortable, like you are interested in him as a person and not a target.

The Holy Spirit can move in a group that's hanging out just as much as He can move in a worship service. The danger with assuming that He works in the same exact way every time with every person is that you are telling God, "*Yeah, sure I know you can do whatever you want, God, but* (wink wink) *I know you're going to be making my son a prophet any day now and so I need to keep testing him for it.*" God doesn't care about our systems for Him to work in. He does what He does. Who are we to limit how He does it?

Without question, there are times and opportunities for shotgun evangelism to young people. If you're going to the streets to spread Jesus, or you feel such a powerful urge to speak His name that you feel you'll explode if you don't, go for it. Far be it from me to muzzle that particular work of the Spirit. My point is that it's not the *only* way to share your faith. God doesn't operate under our rules. He doesn't limit His presence to events where there is prayer and fasting. He can be present with a group of boys launching water balloons, just hanging out.

★ ENCOURAGE RELATIONSHIP BUILDING

We do an event every Thanksgiving called Turkey Bowling. It involves getting a couple of old frozen turkeys and letting the kids attempt to knock down the soda bottle "pins." It draws neighborhood kids in like vultures to a carcass.

At the conclusion of the first Turkey Bowling event, one of the more creative and scientific young men of the group (part Philosopher, part Knucklehead) decided it would be hilarious to grab the soda bottles that had been used as pins and throw them high in the air. This bottle of Coke had been knocked down and shaken up for the better part of two hours so when it collided with the asphalt there was a major explosion. The best part was that the cap came off and soda started shooting out of the end, making the bottle blast over the roof of the gymnasium nearby. NASA couldn't have designed a better propulsion experiment. In case you don't realize just how amazing it was, let me tell you that it sailed completely *over the gym*, which houses two full-sized basketball courts, a skateboarding quarter-pipe, and a kitchen.

Every category of boy on the spectrum went delirious with joy at the sight of that Coke rocket. There were high-fives all around. Kids who at school would walk past each other without even a glance were suddenly working together to figure out a way to make the bottle launch farther the next time.

The next week back in my office I got the idea to have a party for the guys that involved playing video games and launching Coke bottles in the parking lot. I named it "Coke Rocket Halo," after a popular video game where you defend the earth from invading space aliens.

The evening of Coke Rocket Halo arrived and I was shocked to see our youth room crowded with boys. This was a Friday night during the fall in Texas, and normally anyone who plans an event during football season winds up being the only human being there (with all the townsfolk questioning his sanity).

Boys of all shapes and sizes were running amok in the hallways of the church. Jocks were playing foursquare and mini basketball while the rest of them took turns blasting aliens. There was loud music blaring and pizza was disappearing. Somehow, inexplicably, a collection of socks was already strewn about the room.

A Knucklehead got the idea that virtual combat was unsatisfying, so he found a large container of those colored foam pool noodles and smacked his buddy on the head with one. The sound was like a dinner bell, and suddenly every guy in the room was armed with the noodle of his choosing and trying his level best to be Grand Champion of the Noodle Fight Arena.

Aliens being blasted, rubber balls bouncing, noodle combat raging, I watched it all with a dopey smile on my face. I thought about how those boys would be going home the next morning, many of them to places that didn't want them. For one brief night they could get away from their lives with drug addicted mothers or abandoning fathers and just whack each other with noodles. I wasn't about to stop them. They live in a frenzied world of fleeting happiness, here for a moment and then gone as soon as dad beats down the door of the apartment.

In one corner was a kid who once told me his abusive father was going to hunt his mother down. I watched another boy smacking a Moody Musician with a noodle, and then remembered he had recently confessed to suicidal thoughts. Elsewhere were normal kids with no major problems.

I ordered everyone outside for the great spectacle of Coke launching and it didn't disappoint. Their faces were gleeful as each boy took a turn tossing bottles in the air. I watched another guy pick up a cracked container and start drinking the remains of soda from it. His mom and dad recently divorced and were in the middle a fight over who had to take him in.

Not who *wanted* him, but who *had* to take him.

Midway through the night, as the sock piles grew and the alien hordes continued their onslaught, I was making the first of my rounds in the hallway to make sure that no windows were broken and no socks were stuffed in the air ducts. It had been a huge success so far, with the exception of some new stains in the carpet. That wasn't a problem, though, because there are stains older than I am in that carpet.

A young guy that hadn't been coming to our youth group in recent months ran up to me, out of breath. I'll call him Joey.

"Cliff, you got a sec?"

"Sure, bro. What's up?"

"Well, first of all, Brandon bloodied someone's nose with a noodle. It was awesome."

"Is the kid okay? Who was it?" I asked, a little concerned.

"Some kid that some other kid brought. But he's okay because his turn came up in Halo and he's really good and Josh went and got him some toilet paper to stuff up his nose and said he was sorry and stuff."

"Sweet ... You doin' all right?" I asked him as I picked up a sock on the ground.

"Yeah, I guess ... how's Joshua doing?"

He was referring to my two year-old son who had become a popular mascot in the youth group.

"He's doing great, man. He just cut another tooth. Slobbers everywhere."

"That's cool."

Joey kept walking beside me down the hallway. I could tell something was on his mind, but, since he was a full-blooded Knucklehead, I didn't want to rush things. Those kids can be extremely difficult to speak heart to heart with.

"Can I show you something?"

I grabbed the door handle and glanced at him. "You bet, what is it?"

He pulled out his wallet and fumbled around a minute with it. Out came a small photograph which he handed over to me.

I looked at a newborn baby boy, his eyes squinting in the light. Obviously it had been taken in a hospital maternity ward. Cute little fellow.

"Awesome, dude. Who is it?" I asked him as I handed it back.

He didn't reply, so we kept walking back towards the youth room. After a minute he spoke up again.

"I love Halo. It's so fun to get to play it with other people. That one Sprite bottle you threw went so far."

I knew that just walking with only the two of us made him feel uncomfortable. Guys don't have many deep conversations where they weep and look into each other's eyes. We had to stay busy in order for him to open up more.

I walked through the door to the youth room and surveyed the damage from the candy fight. Not too bad. It wouldn't take long in the morning to pick it all up. I would have to make sure everyone stayed until it was done. Our poor maintenance crew always had to get saddled with helping us clean up after every youth event.

I waited for him to speak again as we walked across the room to where the kids were watching the television screens and laughing. I began to pick up candy off the floor and noticed Joey was helping me. He was going through the motions mechanically, lost in thought.

"That was my kid, in that picture. He's my son. We called him Tony. She, my girlfriend, has an uncle or something named Tony."

I kept picking up candy without missing a beat.

"She...we're gonna get married, maybe sometime next spring. I want to make sure she gets a chance to go to college. I don't want her to feel like she has to be stuck at home or something. She's a cool girl, you would really like her. 'Course she wouldn't be able to work at home right away anyway. I mean, not work at home, but be at home with the baby. She was the one who told me to come here tonight and hang out with the guys and play Halo and stuff. This has been awesome, when is the next one?"

Something knotted up in the back of my throat and I was forced to clear it.

"I don't know man, maybe next month. We'll see how it goes." I tried to keep focusing on the candy, and not the fact that Joey was fifteen years old.

"Anyway, I just wanted to let you know. I'm trying to be a man and be strong and stuff, like you said. I was … um … "

At this point he sat up and started fidgeting with a piece of wrapper he'd found on the floor. I was silently praying to find the right words at the right time when Joey spoke up again.

"I know you tell us to make good decisions and to be smart and be a man and stuff. I was really embarrassed to come back here. Not that anyone was going to say anything, everyone's great here. I just … it's kinda weird." He shrugged his shoulders and looked up at a video game screen. "That guy has 47 points, he's gonna win that game."

★ BE WILLING TO LET CHRIST WORK IN DIFFERENT WAYS

Of all the kids in my youth group, Joey was the absolute *last* one that I thought might become a new teen fatherhood statistic. I'd have bet the farm on it. He didn't have a rosy background, but he was a nice kid that was very polite and just awkward enough to be ignored by the most of the girls in the youth room. This is why it is so critical to connect with boys on a level that brings out openness. They may be hiding struggles and conflicts that only burst forth while defending earth from alien invaders.

There are kids who come to that crazy Coke Rocket Halo event who would never step foot through the door of a church. They want nothing to do with church and it doesn't matter how many nice people may be there. When they think of church, they think of boredom. They think of people telling them what to do all the time. They think of the girls giggling in the corner of the youth room that will never be interested in them. They think of their mom or dad dragging them to a different person every week wondering why no one is fixing their kid. They think of all the people who will look down on them for messing up their lives by getting a girl pregnant. So they don't want to come to "church."

But they *will* come blast space aliens.

I described earlier that a boy loves video games because they let him live a virtual life. He doesn't have to be a normal boring kid when he boots up the gaming system. Of all the activities I have ever tried, nothing works as well as video games to create camaraderie among the different categories of boys. Jocks will sit down with Moody Musicians to play the game *Guitar Hero*, where you press buttons in time with a song (we monitor the content). Gangsters will plop on the couch with Knuckleheads to fight it out in Halo. It doesn't matter their background; *everyone* is accepted and liked if they are a fellow "gamer."

Many have said that video games are a waste of time and destroy your brain. I challenge those people to sit down and actually try to solve the puzzles that exist in some of them. I am an educated person, and yet I'll get my clock cleaned by a teenager who is naturally good at math and can easily solve complex game riddles.

There's no question that far too many hours can be wasted playing video games, but instead of just shouting that

fact to them and shutting the console off, give this suggestion a chance: ask them about it. I know that sounds like
torture because you couldn't care less about the fate of virtual
earth, but your son will be shocked if you show an interest
in his world.

Sitting down next to him on the couch and asking him
questions about what he is doing in the game will give him
something to brag to you about. Listen for the pride in his
voice as he describes the high score he just received or the
shot he just made on that alien.

You might be thinking, "Gosh, is this guy saying video
games that have shooting are okay?" It depends. If it's a very
dark game with dark themes, or contains sexually explicit
material, then, of course, it isn't very edifying. But if it's a
military simulator or an alien invasion game, and there's no
vulgar content, then I don't personally believe there is anything wrong with it. I *do* believe that we can be too sen-
sitive in our culture. Using the argument that video games
with fighting are unhealthy, one should also automatically
disqualify games like paintball as well. That's a simulated
combat game but with *real* people involved. Or how about
football? Men crushing each other's bodies for our enter-
tainment. It's a slippery slope to single out video games for
exclusion. In moderation, they're probably all okay.

Teaching boys the way of the warrior used to take place
outside in the woods. Now, with so many absentee fathers,
boys are teaching themselves on a game console in the living room. The public schools got tired of warrior training
and shortened recess time. Medicate them, subdue them, try
your very best to calm them down and they will *still* find

a way to pretend they're making some desperate last stand against overwhelming odds. There are a lot of violent stories in Scripture. And while we should never glorify violence, it doesn't mean that we shy away from it. Samson slaughtered a thousand men with the jawbone of a donkey. God doesn't contradict Himself, so all those war stories in the Bible must have something to tell us.

Becoming a warrior is hugely applauded in Scripture. Don't mistake love of violence with becoming a warrior; the two are very different. A warrior defends the weak, stands up for justice, loves only one woman, and plays with his children. He also hates using physical violence and desires peace.

A powerful conversation between a dad and a son can begin while the boy is saving innocent people as the commander of a virtual Army task force. The dad says, "Son, what's the storyline of this game?" Junior can reply with, "Well dad, you're this Army commander who has to rescue hostages from these terrorists..." Dad can then have a good talk with Junior about the merits of courage and honor and why a man must only use force in certain circumstances.

Yes, boys can become obsessed with games. But they can become obsessed with anything. Singling out video games doesn't seem to be very consistent. On the contrary, I think games make a great starting point to discuss what really matters in life.

Let me explain that a little further. The ultimate goal would be to wean a boy off an *addiction* to video games. But that doesn't mean they should be removed entirely. Like I said before, they can unite guys from all walks of life and create a common ice-breaker. Asking a question about the game will allow a boy to talk about something that he's proud of.

That can lead to conversations about other topics, like school and girls and spirituality. If he senses you genuinely want to get to know him and his world, he might open up to you.

If you condemn everything about video games and tell him to stop wasting his time, he won't have any respect for you because he doesn't think you have any respect for him. It's your right to do it, but it probably won't be effective.

Some of my best conversations with boys about becoming men and living a life of excellence (necessary conversations if they come from fatherless homes) were in the middle of playing a video game. Something about the story or a character in it will inspire me to say, "Hey that's a pretty awesome way of showing what real courage is." I know it doesn't sound like a theological study of Romans, but it's a start.

The video game industry operates a lot like the movie industry. Each game is given a rating: EC (Early Childhood) through AO (Adults Only). There are some in between as well. EC and E (Everyone) are about the equivalent to a G-rated movie. E10 is for everyone 10 and above, and would be equal to a PG movie. T is for Teen rated games and would be the equivalent to a PG-13 movie. M is for Mature and is like an R-rated movie. AO means "Adults Only" and is the same as an NC-17 film.

Hardly any games, especially in the United States, get the AO rating because it would be a commercial disaster. With each rating comes a description of why it was rated that way. Look for the reasons given for the rating when examining a video game box. A game rated "M" can get that rating simply because there is gunfire in it.

Making snap judgments of a game based solely upon its

rating is a mistake, in my opinion. If all R-rated movies were bad, then *The Passion of the Christ* would have been unwatchable for believers in Christ. Therefore, while the ratings can give you an idea, it's good to do the research on your own to find out what a game's content is. Blanket condemnation of a game just because you heard a Christian broadcaster say it has "objectionable content" isn't a very good idea. Maybe that guy's "objectionable content" is merely a storyline that involves non-biblical characters.

A good way of becoming informed is by reading the reviews of games on websites. I write reviews on my own website. There are a lot of other resources available to parents out there. And as I said before, I recommend examining the reasons given for a particular rating. There are some good Christian review sites, but you could also try stopping by a game store and asking the pimple-faced kid behind the counter his opinion of a certain game. That allows you to interact with an indigenous native of modern gaming culture and get another perspective.

Age is a big thing to consider when establishing your position on video games. Boys who are 13 will handle things differently than boys who are 17. There's no question that a game with morally perverse content or images that encourage depression aren't healthy, and you are justified in removing them. But give the other games a chance. Become informed. If you yank away the video games without any explanation and say, "You should stop wasting your life," then you're going to miss something. You're going to miss the cry of his soul looking for a place to vent the warrior within him.

It's important to your son, so it ought to be important to

you. There's something more going on in his heart than just having fun. He's communicating a desire for adventure and excitement to you. Let him try some alternative activities that will be more appealing than just slouching in his room all day. We make our youth boys go out in the nearest set of woods and build dams across rivers. If you can get him outdoors, the natural man in him will eventually connect. It's not a quick fix, but given the proper exposure to other exertions he may not want to play games quite as much.

There's nothing that I have in common with a young man whose parents are on drugs or in jail…except video games. If I can speak that language to him, he'll trust me and listen to me. The two hours of sitting down and firing weapons at gooey creatures pays off when he suddenly says, "Man, life at home really sucks right now." Or, "Cliff, I just became a dad and no one in my family knows about it."

The bond formed among boys while they are having fun is stronger than steel. It's a hill worth dying on to include hanging out in the spiritual activities you do. This is of the utmost importance when dealing with a young man who has never spent time around church or Christians in his life. His first impression of Jesus needs to be one of joy, not condemnation.

He isn't attracted to our arrogant pronunciations about his morally bankrupt life. Introducing him to Christianity by pointing out all that he does wrong doesn't seem to work, I used to try that approach and it failed every time. Instead, as

Paul writes in Galatians 5:1, let him *want* to change his ways when he sees the freedom that Christ offers.

The question to ask yourself is this: is your teenager associating Jesus with fun? You should speak hard truth to them, teach them the rules, and raise them in the way they should go. But never forget the fun. Joey came to us with his heart laid bare because we had formed a common bond with laughter. He associated church with fun and happiness, and in his time of need he wanted to come to us, despite how awkward it was for him. Joey would not have shown up back at church if Coke bottles weren't being launched and he knew that the furious crashing of his life could be eased for a few hours, lost in a shower of soda mist.

SHINE YOUR LIGHT

Situation:

> Boys believe they have to look just like everyone else at church in order to be a Christian.

Mission:

> Show them that they are created to worship God in their own unique way.

Execution:

★ BE CAREFUL OF "CHURCHINESS"

If there is anything that turns boys off of Jesus the most, it has to be "churchiness." Dan Kimball, in his fantastic book *They Like Jesus but not the Church*, describes a phenomena that he dubs the "Christian Bubble." It's the mindset many Christians have that they usually aren't even aware of. They're constantly around Christian friends and do Christian activities and begin to isolate themselves from the people who need the message the most.

I'm going to describe how this affects teen boys by referring to this mindset as "churchiness." Let me define it for you with an illustration so that there's no misunderstanding. We'll use the example of an imaginary guy named Bill. Bill is a really nice fellow and is devoted to the Lord. He has a loving wife named Elizabeth, and they have several kids.

When Bill wakes up in the morning, his alarm clock is set to the local Christian radio station. He gets his jogging clothes on and plugs in the earphones of his music player where he starts playing Christian hits. For a brief moment he considers the oldie rock station, but then remembers that Christians can't listen to any of that.

When Bill returns to the house from his run, Elizabeth and the kids are sitting happily around the table preparing for the day. Bill showers and sits down to eat breakfast with the family. They pray together and then depart. So far, so good.

Bill arrives at work, where he quickly walks over to the other Christian in his department and they start to talk about yesterday's sermon. "Man, that preacher really brought it, it was *awesome!*" He tries telling the guy at the water fountain, but he didn't seem to care.

Bill goes back to his office thinking about all of the guys that he wishes would come to church next Sunday. The pastor is preaching on humility, and Bill knows plenty of people in the office who need to hear that message.

At coffee break time, Bill gathers with his Christian buddies and they talk about the men's retreat this next weekend. They look around at the other office workers and talk about how all of those guys could benefit from a men's retreat, because, wow, that preacher who's coming can really bring it!

At the end of the day, Bill drives home with the Christian station on and once again trying to ignore the classic rock station. He wonders about his son's new interest in a band that isn't Christian, and worry kicks into him. Why can't that kid see that Jesus needs to be the focus of his life? He arrives home, kisses his wife and tussles the heads of the kids. At the dinner table he notices that his son is distant and a little moody.

"Son, what's the problem over there?"

Doug, the son, fiddles with his spaghetti a minute and then mutters, "Oh, nothing."

"No, come on, tell us! How was your day?" Awkward pause.

"Um...well...we were talking about evolution in science class today, and the teacher really said a lot of stuff that made sense, you know, about how it's got all this evidence and stuff."

"So what did you do?"

His son looks away. "I didn't say anything, I didn't really know what to say."

Ah, a teachable moment, Bill thinks to himself.

"Son, the next time that teacher tells you baloney like that, tell him that the Bible is pretty clear about evolution. It's terrible. You need to speak the truth in love."

Doug fidgets some more. "The thing is, dad, I don't think those people really care what the Bible thinks. They think it's just full of contradictions and myths and that if you take it literally, you aren't very smart."

"That's crazy, son. Tell them that the Bible is the Word of God, useful in all things. Just quote the Scripture to them, they'll eventually understand."

The young man fiddles some more and says, "I don't think that's going to work."

Bill can't disguise the frustrated look on his face. Why doesn't Doug just *get* it?

The day began similarly for Elizabeth. After Bill left, she

got the kids to school and headed for her own session at the gym. The Christian music in her iPod really got her fired up, and she posted her best time on the treadmill ever. She used to listen to the oldies love song station, but since it was what she listened to before she got saved, it wasn't holy enough anymore.

Walking out to the car in the parking lot, she opens the trunk of the van, putting her hand on the bumper sticker that reads, "Hell is a Hot Place." She drives away and immediately calls up one of her friends so that they can start planning for the women's Bible study on Thursday. Once inside the grocery store she stands in line next to a bunch of other women and thinks of ways to invite them to come to the Bible study.

She finally mentions this to one of them, a nice looking young gal who smiles and asks, "Hi … did I catch your name?"

"Elizabeth!" she replies sweetly. "My husband Bill and I attend a church on Simpson Boulevard that I really think you would enjoy coming to. We have a women's Bible study on Thursday that would heal the brokenness in your soul."

The woman looks back at her politely and says, "My name is Tara. We're new in town and don't really know anyone. Do you know where I could find out how to get around the city? I get so lost and those freeways are intimidating-"

Elizabeth smiles and interrupts her. "If you come to our women's Bible study, we really address matters of the heart. A good place to find a city map is on that rack over there. Do you know Jesus, by the way?"

Tara looks a little embarrassed and says, "I went to church when I was a kid, but my husband and I aren't that religious. We go on Easter and Christmas sometimes, but that's about it. So…um…you were saying that the rack in the corner has some good city maps in it?" Elizabeth senses her opportunity. "God is the center of all we do. You need to come to our Bible study and hear about all the wonderful things He does. The lady who leads the study is anointed with the Holy Spirit, you just have to see it!"

The checkout line starts to shorten, so Tara looks awkwardly back and forth between the cashier and Elizabeth. "Well, it was nice to meet you, thanks for the tip on the city map."

"Oh, not a problem, and I will be praying that you can make it to the women's Bible study!"

Arriving back at home, Elizabeth prepares the meal and her thoughts drift to Tara from the grocery store. *Poor girl, I hope she can make it to the Bible study. I would hate to not ever see her again. If I could just get her to church…*

As the family gathers for dinner, Elizabeth listens to the dialogue between her son and husband. She, too, can't understand why her son is so unwilling to take a stand in front of his peers. She jumps in after Bill's statement about the Word of God. "That's right, son. Even today, God gave me an opportunity to witness to a lady in the grocery store checkout line. I was telling her all about Jesus and how much He loved her and she seemed to really be responding. I think she's going to come to the women's Bible study to learn even more."

Their son's day is quite different. Doug arrives at school early and attends the campus Bible study. It was okay, though he'd heard that same message dozens of times. As he walks out of the classroom he overhears some of the other kids talking about the concert on Friday night that will be held at the church on Simpson Boulevard. Supposedly this

Christian rock band sounds *just like* that secular rock band that the lost kids listen to, so it's gonna be awesome!

Doug shrugs his shoulders and thinks to himself that the band isn't all that great, they're usually just copycatting the secular band. Of course, he can't tell his mom that because she'll think he hates God or something.

His day is pretty uneventful. Lunch was cool, some kind of tater-tot thing. At the table next to him he listens to some of the kids talk about the band that will be in concert at the civic center. He remembers bitterly that his parents wouldn't let him attend *that* concert because it wasn't a Christian band. They'd ordered him to attend the concert at the church.

As he walks into science class and plops into his desk he notices that the teacher has a painting of some sort of half-man thing hanging on the wall. The sound of rustling papers and kids laughing fills the silence before the teacher walks in. Doug listens as the teacher begins to describe evolution to them, about how there was a bang, and a tadpole became a monkey, and so on. He throws in a reference to the possibility that God kick-started evolution and that you don't have to be an atheist to believe evolution took place.

There's something uneasy in Doug's conscience as he listens to this. There are a lot of gaps and problems with what the teacher is saying, but he doesn't know how he would bring it up. The other kids seem to be taking it okay, writing notes and stuff. Suddenly in the back a hand raises.

The teacher looks over the top of his reading glasses. "Yes?"

"Excuse me, but the Bible clearly states that God created the heavens and the earth, so evolution can't be true."

The science teacher smiles politely and replies, "As I said

before, you can believe in God and also believe in evolution. There's nothing in the Bible that says God couldn't use evolution to bring about different species."

The young lady who had spoken the question answered, "No, the Bible is very clear about it. Evolution can't take place."

Doug wonders in his head where in the Bible it actually says that.

There are snickers, and the teacher says, "Then how do you explain the change from light skin to darker skin when exposed to sunlight? That's considered a form of evolution. Only one form of evolution involves changes from one species to another. Other types of evolution are minor and take place all around us every day. Are you saying that you don't get sunburned after staying in the sun?"

"Um, no."

Doug was listening to this very intently. The girl talking was the head of the campus Bible study and she was arrogantly making a fool of herself in front of all these kids. He hoped someone didn't figure out that he went to that Bible study.

She spoke again, "I just think that before you tell all of us that evolution is true, you need to understand more of the Bible."

The science teacher is kind and replies, "Thank you for your input, I appreciate your interest."

At the dinner table that night, Doug is really struggling with the evolution thing. He knows that a lot of smart guys in sweater vests have written smart books about it from a creation standpoint; maybe he should look into those. Maybe his dad might know some...

But instead, his dad is looking at him with disappointment.

How do I explain to my dad that if I just quote Bible verses in science class, I am going to look like an idiot?

He listens to his mom's story, and it really hurts him. How come she has so much success sharing her faith? His dad seems to have a lot of success because he talks a lot about all the guys at the office who are responding to his testimony.

Doug believes in God and knows Jesus, but why is it that other Christians at school and church have to try so hard to be ... irritating?

There's a lot in that little fake story that I could spend some time on, but I will narrow it down to how it affects teenagers. It's a compilation of a bunch of different scenarios that I have personally witnessed or observed go on in many Christian families.

No specific thing that either Bill or Elizabeth did was wrong at face value. Perhaps they were a little abrasive and shallow, but they were good, decent people who genuinely wanted to let people know about their church. Which was exactly their problem.

At some point in their Christian walk, the focus became more about the social connections and arrangements made through church than living a daily walk with Jesus. Church became a hobby. Let me declare that church is a really lame hobby. Seriously, buy a time share membership or go golfing, but don't make church a hobby.

Reading through the Gospel accounts of Jesus' ministry while on earth, it would appear that He had quite a different idea about how we were to be among those in the world. He visited the homes of Jewish tax collectors. This was double treachery. Not only were these guys making money for the hated Roman occupiers, but they were also making it off the backs of their fellow Jews. There was no more hated person in Jewish society, and Jesus actually went out of His way to be with them.

Prostitutes, sinners, or tax collectors; anyone was able to be in His presence. He didn't support their behavior and spoke to them about the need to repent, but incredibly enough, people actually liked being around Him.

That's the key. They *liked* Him. He was "teaching them as one having authority" (Matthew 7:29), but they also just liked Him. He was approachable and easy to be around. He wanted to get to know the people He created and not just bombard them with religious rules. Something about Jesus that we can forget is that many times He only delivered a message when someone asked Him a question. He knew the lost would come seeking for Him because He promised they would.

People like Bill and Elizabeth really truly mean well, but I do believe they're unaware of the damage they are inflicting to their teenage son's view of Christianity. Instead of encouraging him to reason and probe for his own answers, they order him to stop asking questions. When he wants to experience something all his buddies are doing, they shoot it down right away because it isn't labeled "Christian." Here, fair or not, are Doug's conclusions after being raised in that environment:

> I am never to hang out with Lost Kids.
> I am never to listen to any secular music.
> I am never to have any social life outside of church.

I am never to talk about anything other than church
with Lost Kids.
I am never…
I am never…
I am never…

A depressing thing starts to happen. God becomes the old
man on the throne who hands out His list of "nevers," and
Doug believes that *not* doing stuff is what makes God happy.
If our holiness before God is judged entirely upon what we
don't do, then I have to wonder what we think appeals to
young men about that. It sure as a monkey's uncle doesn't
appeal to me.

That makes me want to walk out of church, slam the
door, and never go in again. And it's exactly what millions
are doing.

★ BE HATED FOR THE RIGHT REASONS

Jesus told his followers that they would be persecuted and
hated by all men on account of His name. So that begs the
question: how are we hated? It's a wonderful badge of honor
to be hated on account of Christ's name. He promised us in
Matthew 10:22 that if we are sold-out following Him, the
entire world will hate us. Not exactly the stuff of a pep rally,
but those who know Jesus understand why it's so motivat-
ing. If we're hated by the world that means we are following
Jesus. A life of total obedience to Christ is one that cares
nothing for the opinion of the world. It's Jesus at all costs.

There has been a misunderstanding of that passage, however. True, it says we are going to be hated. But why? On account of His name.

So I then pose another question: Are we hated on account of His name, or are we just hated?

The lie that has been told to teenage boys is that to be a Christian you have to lose all of your own identity, lose all of your old friends, and walk around converting people in an obnoxious manner. You have to be that kid in the back of the class who doesn't engage in any discussion and spews out a lot of verses.

Part of what we can do as parents, youth leaders, whatever you are, is to make sure that young men know they're *not* supposed to change who they are. The old self filled with sin must change, but the aspects and gifts of every personality are given by God. They really are special and unique snowflakes, despite what I tell the kids on Wednesday nights.

Churchiness, and not Jesus, has become the focus for many Christians. Bill ignored all the guys at work who weren't fellow Christians and yet claimed to be making an impact in his office. Elizabeth didn't stop talking about her church's Bible study long enough to catch that Tara was lonely and just wanted to chat with someone. They hang out with Christian friends, listen to Christian music, do social gatherings where only other Christians attend, and speak with really scary religious language.

I don't believe that most Christians desire to be viewed that way, but we haven't exactly done the best job of preventing it. There are many times we are not hated on account of His name—we're just hared.

When this is happening, teenage boys are fully aware of

it. They can be easily embarrassed when other Christians preen their feathers and announce that everyone else's faults need to be pointed out. They have a hard time understanding why the Christian community goes into an uproar over a professional athlete who fathers a child out of wedlock, as though a person who doesn't know Christ is expected to live like he does.

We also tend to make it a point to present ourselves as intellectually incompetent. There are many arguments over the years that Christians have used in order to prove the reality of God. Most are solid, but there are a few that have become little more than urban legend.

I used to toss false arguments out there like hand grenades and assume they were authoritative, and God mercifully spared me from being called on it.

Only the Word is authoritative and should be tossed like a hand grenade (albeit a tactically and skillfully tossed hand grenade).

The point of this is not to claim that creation science arguments are useless. There has been undeniably powerful research done that indicates a Creator. What I'm suggesting is that it does our cause no service to use arguments and claims that are demonstrably false. Theology degrees are not biology degrees. If we are ever to be taken seriously in academic circles we have to come to the place of honesty in debate. Remember that our faith doesn't depend on perfect natural evidence, but rather the evidence of the Holy Spirit and the evidence that God chose to leave for us written into the earth, as it says in Romans 1.

I hear a lot of confusion regarding the evolution issue

among teen guys, and not just the ones who attend public schools, so let me take a minute to clear up some of it,
and help you understand the types of things they are hearing
about.

Evolution comes in two forms: *micro*evolution and *macro*evolution. Microevolution is demonstrated fact. To deny it is utter
foolishness. Surprised I would say that? Try out this experiment: put down this book and go stand outside in the backyard. Don't apply any sunscreen. If you remain outside for an
entire day (assuming there is sunshine) you will undergo the
micro evolutionary process of sun-burning. I have skin that
mutates into lobster red when I spend too much time in the
sun. I experience this microevolution frequently in the cursed
south Texas heat. Microevolution is simply the observable
change in a species over a short period of time.

The one to watch out for is macroevolution. This is the
whole ape-became-a-man thing. It's also the one that lacks
any verifiable proof for having ever occurred, despite naturalist claims to the contrary.

The sentence at many Christian dinner tables, "Son,
evolution is false because the Bible says so," is a thoroughly
incorrect statement. The Bible never once addresses the subject. Ironically, the concept of evolution is heartily endorsed
by Scripture. Evolution simply means change over time.
The word "evolution" has been adopted by naturalist think-
ers and transformed into always relating to physical species.
Scripture would define evolution as growing in the knowledge and experience of God.

I experienced an evolution in my heart and mind when I came to a saving knowledge of Christ. My skin evolves slowly over time in that south Texas sunlight. Not all evolution is false, so we do better to define the terms of the discussion before stamping our self-righteous feet and smugly proclaiming it to be.

All right, this isn't science class, so I won't continue to press the point, but you need to understand the damage shutting down our brains can cause. If you don't think a teenage boy picks up on the ignorance of the Christian community then you need to spend some more time talking with him. I will cover this subject more in chapter 9.

We're all guilty of heartless evangelism, myself included. I can remember the days when I would meet someone new, listen to them for a few minutes, and then try and figure out a way to work the Gospel message in. I didn't care about simply getting to know them. I didn't want to actually listen to their reply when I said, "What's up?"

I was always looking for my angle, that little sentence they would utter that I saw as my opportunity to attack like an Evangelism Shark:

Me: "Hey, dude, what's up?"

Innocent Bystander: "Not much."

Me: "Cool…Hey, you know 2,000 years ago they didn't think Jesus was that much either."

Innocent Bystander: "…um…okay…"

We can discuss my evangelism techniques another time. The point was I never showed a real interest in people because I was too busy looking for "the angle." The "angle" is the desire to make someone act like us because we are too insecure to accept people for who they are. The motivation is not people coming to Jesus; it's getting people into church.

That might not be you, so to you I say this: breathe the hope that is in Christ night and day, and shine your light for all to see. But never substitute that holy fire with the uncaring motive of assimilation. We have Good News for the world to hear; we're not sculpting them into a mindless society of do-gooders.

If you aren't truly sincere in your efforts at telling a young man about Jesus, be aware that there's nothing a teenager can spot as fast as a phony. A poser, they will call you. A poser, they will call you. My former youth pastor gave me some of the best advice I ever received:

"Don't be fake. Just be yourself. They'll be able to tell the difference."

And he was exactly right. It was only a couple weeks into my Cool-Youth-Pastor-Guy phase at church that I got called on it by one of the kids. He told me stop being a poser because they liked me the way I was. Ouch.

Many boys have complained to me about their parent's "fake Christianity." I try to tell them that it's not necessarily "fake" just because they make mistakes. They're only human like the rest of us. The problem, comes the reply, is that no mistakes are ever admitted to.

Nothing—let me repeat it again—*nothing* will ruin a boy's view of God like a set of parents who demand obedience to God's commandments and then don't follow through with it themselves.

If mistakes get made, and there isn't any repentance, then

that is precisely how they will view Jesus. "He must not be real, because if *these* arrogant people are His servants, then there must not be anything real about Him." Who wants to follow a harsh master with ruthless demands of perfection? If your desire is to see him love Jesus with the same passion that you love Jesus, it's gotta come from his own heart.

Your son will notice if you are phony. He takes very good mental notes about you. Parents tend to think they can hide their troubles from their kids, and maybe sometimes they can. Not as much as they wish, though. So I would say to just be yourself. Warts and all. An honest struggle in a walk with Christ is much better for him to see than a false religion of rules. He will respect your honesty, even if he doesn't show it, and things might go better in your relationship with him.

★ BE A CAMPFIRE, NOT A SPOTLIGHT

In the old Star Trek television series, there was a race of enemies known as the Borg. The Borg went around from galaxy to galaxy destroying worlds and "assimilating" all of the inhabitants. In Star Trek lingo, this meant that everyone was going to be turned into a replica of the Borg prototype, and everyone was going to look, talk, and act in exactly the same way. Their famous line was, "You will be assimilated. Resistance is futile."

One of the biggest false assumptions that plague young people is the idea that when you become a believer in Christ you have to drop everything about your personality and become assimilated into the Borg. You can only have Christian friends, only listen to Christian music, and only go to Christian schools. If you violate any of these rules, then you are living in sin.

That's an extreme representation of what most Christians believe, but we need to realize that it's how teenagers view it. Guys are running away from church in droves because they think that they will be forced to abandon their skateboard or CD collection. That view is reinforced when we as the church body look down on every kid that walks in with his ears pierced or is wearing a black hooded sweatshirt.

Jesus told His followers in Matthew 5 that they were to shine their light before all men in order that people would see their good deeds and glorify the Father in heaven. There is a common misinterpretation of this verse, however. The Greek words "humon" and "phos" are what Matthew used to record how Jesus said "Let your light" during this sermon.

The better way to understand that in English is "shine your light," since the pronoun involved is more urgent than the English suggests. The difference would be simply opening a doorway and letting some light from the hall spill into a darkened room, or walking into the darkened room and turning a flashlight on. One of those is merely letting light fall in, the other is actively turning on a light from inside the source of darkness.

Here's how this relates. We have permission from Jesus to shine our light to all mankind. Some of us are spotlights and want to blast a two million candlepower beam into the faces of everyone around. Others are gentle candles, warmly beckoning people to come and relax in the warm glow. Both sources of light are effective at removing darkness. In John 1, Jesus is described as the Light and that the darkness does not overcome the Light. On the Damascus Road, Jesus used a two million candlepower spotlight to mess up Paul's world and bring him back from the darkness. There are plenty of times that the spotlight is necessary to fully illuminate the areas of darkness.

In South Texas we have cockroaches the size of cats. I'm only partly kidding about this. They're huge. When you walk into a room and flick on the fluorescent light, you can see the cockroaches go scrambling. They hate light. In the same way, evil will flee when exposed to the light of Jesus.

But the spotlight isn't the only way to bring light into a dark room. In the Matthew 5 passage, Jesus makes the comparison to a lamp stand, warmly beckoning all who stumble blindly in the darkness. I think of a campfire in the woods that you can see guiding you through the black depths of the forest. Branches keep tearing at your face, you lost the trail a long time ago, there are scary noises all around, and when you see that campfire you want to cry out in relief.

The postmodern teenage boy is usually in search of the campfire, not the spotlight. I've noticed that too much smash-mouth evangelism can turn them off or scare them away. They feel, rightly or wrongly, as though you don't really care about them as a person, only a target for conversion.

When I was in high school, I had some buddies who would wait on top of the roof during Halloween and try to scare the little kids that were trick-or-treating. Either they would scream like banshees as the children approached, or they'd throw water balloons down on them. It was cruel, and the results of their efforts were little children running in terror. The same effect is had on people who don't know Christ and are wary of church things. We don't intend any harm to them but we can treat them like they are bait fish being chomped up by a hammerhead.

Boys, like all of us, need to associate Jesus with happiness and joy, refuge from the cold, and light in the darkness. Kids that are buried in despair can be resentful about having the spotlight shown on them; but show them a candle and they may slowly start to soften up.

★ LET THEM SHINE THEIR OWN LIGHT

All boys have something they can shine their light in. Jocks can play sports like God gifted them to. Gangsters can use their leadership ability to positively influence others. Musicians can smash those guitars or drums and praise the Lord, even if it isn't a "Christian song." Knuckleheads can do knuckle-headed things like firing Coke rockets and bring in fellow Knuckleheads who don't know Jesus. Melting pots can find their identity in Jesus and not in trying to become the Alpha Male of a category, if only we would pull back and let them.

Philosophers love to examine and probe, so we should encourage them. If we know that Jesus is Truth, then He will withstand their scrutiny. We don't need to bury our questions; God wants us to reason together like He said in Isaiah 1:18. The worst way to handle a doubting young man is to get angry and tell him to stop doubting. All that serves to do is make him think you're hiding something from him, causing him to doubt even more. His own search for truth ought to inspire us to take the time to speak with him, and not wave a fork in his face at dinner and say falsehoods like the Bible forbidding evolution.

So the message to teen guys should be, "Shine your light," and not "Stop doing that!" They can be themselves; they have permission just like you to resist the Borg. They're beautiful and unique snowflakes. If they understand that God made them exactly how they are to be as goofily special as they are, then church becomes the inviting campfire, and although they may *dress* like cockroaches, they won't scatter away when the light hits them.

There's a group of neighborhood boys that hang out behind our church's gym. They love to skateboard. I have no skill of any kind on a skateboard, but there are other guys here who love Jesus *and* love to skateboard. They let their light shine on the skateboarding ramp.

There are levels of maturity that a believer in Jesus should strive for, but if something isn't specified in the Scriptures, or it doesn't cause any moral stumbling, then it isn't worth fighting over. How you were called by the Holy Spirit is different than how other people were called. Some were found by Him while they were in jail; some are beckoned through their academic research. The most famous of these is a little-known author named C.S. Lewis. Perhaps you've heard of him. He came to the conclusion, after much academic study and research, that Christ was who He said He was. Lewis even described himself as a dejected initial convert, because he realized he'd been wrong about God his entire life. C.S. Lewis's salvation testimony is no more or less valid than the homeless drug addict who got saved in jail. God simply worked differently with each of them, just like He works differently with boys.

We shouldn't project some of the personal convictions about how God works that we may have onto others. There are plenty of issues in our hypersensitive church culture that are nothing more than differences of opinion, and not 'thus saith the Lord' commandments. Snuffing out the light of a young believer because it doesn't fit our preconceived notion of "being a Christian" is one of the most irresponsible things we can do to younger generations.

LANGUAGE BARRIER

Situation:
> Adults and boys have a serious problem communicating about God.

Mission:
> Establish common language that is easily understood by teenagers.

Execution:

★ LEARN THE NATIVE TONGUE

Scripture says, "For the word of God is living and active and sharper than any two-edged sword, and piercing as far as the division of soul and spirit, of both joints and marrow, and able to judge the thoughts and intentions of the heart" (Hebrews 4:12).

Verses like that one make it clear the Word of God is sufficiently powerful for every situation in life. That being said, allow me to throw out a suggestion: the physical act of quoting Scripture does not guarantee that a person's heart will become softened. Firing off verses like a machine gun isn't the best approach with the majority of teens.

Satan, when he was tempting Jesus, bombarded Him with a bunch of Scripture as well, but it would be hard to make the argument that he got the results he wanted. There's a belief among some Christians that forcing Scripture memorization on a young person is sufficient discipleship. The thought is that in order to be an effective evangelist one has to quote verses continuously in every encounter with an unbeliever. This puts an incredible amount of strain on churchgoing teenagers and is not even consistent with what the Bible itself actually says.

In Acts 17, we find that Paul has made his way to Athens and is waiting for his companions to arrive so they can continue their missionary journey. While "hanging out" in the city, he notices all of the idols that people have been worshipping in order to protect themselves from calamities.

At some point he discovers a simple idol that is engraved with the words, "To an unknown God." Intrigued by this, he makes his way to the part of the city where ideas are debated and starts to engage the pagan philosophers. They are impressed enough to invite him to a place called the Aeropagus. While in this forum Paul gave a speech for the ages, dazzling the intellectuals gathered there with a methodical argument for the truth of the gospel. It's just as shocking for what it does *not* contain, however.

Instead of lengthy quotations from an Old Testament prophet or the Law of Moses, Paul begins by complimenting the Athenians on their religious devotion. He tries to point out that they're looking for the right thing in the wrong places. He tells about the wonders of nature and the evidence of design as proof that there is a God. Man has a general knowledge of God, Paul argues, and people would be able to grasp Him if they only tried to seek Him. Then, surprisingly, Paul quotes some of their own poets as being on the right track in their search for God.

The first thing to notice about how Paul handles the Athenians is that he is friendly and cordial to them. There isn't any bashing over the head with a hammer. He engages them and demonstrates an interest in their ideas, even though he believes they are false. Paul built a bridge to the people so they would be receptive to his own remarks. The Evangelism Shark didn't have to bite his victims in half in order to be effective.

★ SPEAK THE NATIVE TONGUE

The second thing to notice is that Paul speaks in a language that's understandable to his audience. He doesn't quote any prophets because he knows that nobody there would recognize them. In fact, he goes a step further and quotes pagan Greek poets in an effort to demonstrate that the proof about Jesus is evident everywhere. Even those who have the details wrong still search for God. Paul wants to encourage them in their search and point them in the right direction—towards Christ.

If the belief is that Scripture must be quoted every time the Gospel is shared, then we need to deal with the contradiction that this passage of the Bible presents. It is important to remember that during the early centuries of the church there were no copies of Scripture floating around. People relied on the power of the Spirit to spread what was known as The Way. It's a simple message, and they used simple language.

We Christians have way of frightening people off when we encounter them outside of a church building. We use scary words like "anointing" and "spirit-filled" in casual conversation and it can make teenagers very uncomfortable. I'll find myself doing it without even meaning to, especially since I work at a church and am around Christians all day long. Some of the sentences and phrases we use are common language easily understood by folks in the church, but couldn't be more bizarre when someone else hears it.

For example, the following statement would be considered normal inside many church buildings: "That service was very powerful. The pastor was clearly anointed and the presence of the Holy Spirit really filled the room. I pray that the blood of the Lamb washes away the sin in people's lives."

Now, that sentence makes sense if you are a believer in Jesus Christ. If you aren't, then you'd think that the person saying it was a member of some secret cult. Anointing? Spirits filling a room? Washing people with lamb's blood, what? Much of that can't be comprehended by a person who doesn't have a relationship with Jesus or is familiar with church vocabulary. The Christians who speak in such ways usually don't mean anything negative by it; they don't realize they're speaking what is a foreign language to many. That's why it is so important to communicate in terms that are easily understood by those outside the church.

There's a language barrier between modern teens and those in positions of authority over them and it's exactly like the barrier in every other previous generation. What the older generations say doesn't make sense to the teenagers, and vice versa. Quite a bit of conflict can occur simply by miscommunication. So what we need to do is come up with ways to speak to boys that won't produce a blank stare (it'll be tough, since blank stares are pretty much all you get anyway, except when you're talking about pizza or burritos).

For example, to communicate the concept of authority, I tell the kids about Coffee Cup Guy. When they grow up and get jobs, there will always be a guy holding a coffee cup who tells them what to do. It doesn't matter what job it is, be it white collar or blue collar. One day they themselves might get to be Coffee Cup Guy, and, if they work hard, they may earn the right to be the one sipping aromatic brew while telling those under them what to do.

Sometimes Coffee Cup Guy is fair and just. Sometimes he's only using his position of authority to get ahead of everyone else. God allows him to be Coffee Cup Guy because Coffee Cup Guy is a tiny part in God's cosmic plan and has a role to play. All authority, including Coffee Cup Guy, is established by God and we are to be content with it.

Authority is a tricky concept to communicate no matter what you try. You sort of have to just experience it. Civilians tend to think that on a military base the General has all the sway, but that's only partly true. He commands the armies and manages a staff, but it's his wife that has the sway. All his wife has to do is drive through the front entrance of the base, notice the barren parade field, and think to herself, *Wouldn't a Christmas tree look lovely out there this year?* She goes home and tells her husband, who tells his aide the next day that his wife wants a Christmas tree on the parade field. Immediately, 40 soldiers are sent to work constructing a Christmas tree with Army-enforced holiday cheer. Authority in action. (I have no actual proof this was what took place, but when you're one of a dozen disgruntled G.I.'s tasked with setting up a Christmas tree in the middle of the parade field, conspiracy theories help pass the time.)

On subject of how to explain the Holy Spirit, I usually try to describe His as a "covering," a covering that a person wears in order to be protected, to feel safe nuzzled into, and to rely upon in order to accomplish a task. The covering is wild, mysterious, and gentle all at the same time. There is a reason that the Spirit was described as a raging fire throughout the Scriptures, because He is an unstoppable force that cannot be controlled, and yet the tenderness is evident every time a person takes refuge in Him during times of trial. This seems to make sense to boys, who don't really care about how tender and gentle the Holy Spirit is until they need it (as with most men).

So when we use the word "anointing", commonly found in more evangelical or charismatic churches, we need to take the time to explain what precisely is meant by it. It is really hard to get angry with someone who is not a biochemist and does not know what a chlorofluorocarbon is. Likewise, it doesn't necessarily imply that a person does not know or care about Jesus without being familiar with the term "anointing."

There's another way to think about the language barrier, and it's by picturing yourself stranded in Africa. You walk around frantically trying to communicate with someone about your situation, but all they understand is that you are loud and are waving your arms around a lot. No English word makes sense to them, and when they start to talk, none of the local dialect makes sense to you. If someone were to run up to you and start screaming that there was a lion on the edge of the village, you could understand that something was wrong but wouldn't know what it was.

By the concern in your voice and the emotions you show, a teenage guy can detect that you think something is wrong with him. He won't always understand exactly what that is because he doesn't understand your language. Overcoming the language barrier is critical when dealing with young men. If they've been raised in church, they might be familiar with the lingo we toss around. Most kids, though, don't have a clue what we are talking about when we say "Spirit-filled."

★ CHOOSE WELL YOUR HILLS TO DIE ON

To explain this, I will use the example of music, although it could be the same for television or movies.

Music is a language that is completely misunderstood between the generations. It's always been that way. I'm sure someday the musical pendulum will swing back to more easy listening tunes, and when my generation gets older, we'll probably be complaining about all the gentle-sounding stuff being played in worship services. Churches love to fight over worship, unfortunately.

Simply labeling something "Christian music" doesn't automatically qualify it as superior to all other music. Christ can be glorified through secular songs even though the people singing them may not be believers in Jesus. Leonardo da Vinci was strongly anti-Christian, but that didn't mean he was any less of a master painter. If you go to a national park in Montana, you can't consider it to be ugly just because it's managed by the federal government (although it's tempting). God grants gifts to people so that *He* will be glorified, not them. He raises men up and brings them down all to suit His purposes. As He told Pharaoh in Exodus 9:16, "For this reason I have allowed you to remain." Similarly, he anoints people with a gifting that they can either praise Him for or use for selfish means. Either way, He is responsible for giving them that gift.

To condemn all music that isn't labeled "Christian" from your son's music library sets your house up for unnecessary tension. Even worse is condemning a band that is actually a Christian band simply because they sound like they were just thrown into the leopard cage at the zoo, or sell t-shirts that resemble what a toddler would do with ketchup and a blank canvas. The music a boy is listening to is a good window into his soul, so instead of yanking the CD and asking questions later, try starting out with the asking-questions part. If you complain about having nothing to talk to your son about and never ask him about his music, then you're shooting yourself in the foot. He's communicating something to you. Slamming the CD book shut or taking the iPod won't mean anything unless you let him know why you are doing it.

Maintaining the belief that music has to be labeled "Christian" in order to be enjoyed rules out any oldies, love songs, bluegrass, country or classical that we may be listening to. It isn't fair to proclaim rock music of the devil and then switch on the non-Christian oldies station. Your son will notice that, it's a guarantee.

It's also a guarantee that you will never be able to convince him that gospel quartets are better than the band he has in his CD player. There's nothing wrong with gospel quartets;

however, I have yet to see any interest in them among teen-age boys.

Substituting his music with your music rarely works, but it's true that if he was exposed to more positive bands with similar styles he may find them intriguing. You can't force it, though.

As you might suspect, a lot of the music that boys listen to isn't very edifying. If the songs are suicidal, contain mor-ally compromising lyrics or crass language, they clearly aren't beneficial to him. Many bands get a bad reputation unfairly, though, because they "sound like wickedness," as a parent informed me one time. I would suggest careful research before making such a proclamation.

Parents, as always, are fully within their rights to remove anything from their house that they want. I'm not disputing that. I'm suggesting that you ask questions about the band, investigate them, and give an informed reason as to why he is or is not allowed to listen to them anymore. Your son may throw a hissy fit, he may shout that you just don't understand anything, but he will respect you for at least speaking to him like a man. I frequently hear them admit as much.

Legend has it that during the Korean War, a Marine general with the Marine General-sounding name of Chesty Puller called his officers around a map and pointed out their current position. Looking up at them, he said, "Gentlemen, we are outnumbered and surrounded, and our supply has been depleted. I would like you all to pick the hill you are going to die on." What we mean by this nowadays is that not every single issue in your house is a hill to die on. You don't have to defend every blade of grass like it's the difference between your son going to heaven or hell. A moral last stand doesn't have to be made over the fact that your offspring wants to get a bone pierced through his nose like some Stone Age caveman. You can prevent him from doing so (and save him a great deal of pain), but be gentle about it.

Likewise, if he wants to shave his head into quadrants, why not go ahead and let him? Your hair took on a life utterly its own back in the day, and was it really the deciding factor in your knowledge of Christ?

Picking the dying hills with your teenager is hard, there's no getting around it. Nothing I can say here will make it any easier because only you know your son. With that in mind, here are some ideas:

Pray without ceasing. Night and day, drench him in prayer. It's the only proven effective formula. God created him and would love to offer you some advice on raising him. Be prepared, though, for Him to work in a way that could make you uncomfortable. Moses spent forty years in the palaces of Egyptian pagans, but I think it's safe to say he amounted to something. God prepared him in His own time.

Don't get so worked up. He may be driving you absolutely insane, but blowing up at him won't get you anywhere. You'll only get angrier and he will only get more obnoxious.

Engage him. Use language that he can understand, but don't try to speak teenage lingo. You'll sound goofy. Just speak honestly with him. Ask him about video games, sports, music, whatever he's interested in. By asking a lot of questions, he'll realize that you're actually interested in his world.

Establish your authority in a way that makes sense to him. You can only demand obedience from your son during the time he lives in your house. If he obeys all of your rules and then promptly ruins his life as soon as he moves out, then you only succeeded in forcing him to do things that made you look like a good parent to all your friends. His heart went unreached.

The best way to establish authority to a teenage boy is by building a foundational relationship with him. Showing an interest in his world and affirming him there. By doing that you gain influence, and with influence he might better recognize your authority. As he gets older, your relationship moves from one of authority to one of influence anyway. He's preparing to be his own man and you need to be helping him along.

A teenage boy's relationship with Jesus must be *his* relationship with Jesus. It can't be mom and dad's. It can't be a youth pastor's. It must be *his* relationship. He needs to be drawn to Christ, not force-fed Him. There is nothing exciting about joining a cult of rule-makers, and they will hate the thought of becoming like the Borg.

Strip away the misconceptions about who Jesus is, and He will excite them more than pizza and Dr. Pepper ever could. And that's saying something. There is no single method of sharing your faith. That's the beauty of Paul's encounter at the Aeropagus. God will endlessly shock you with His creativity in spreading the news about Himself.

So relax, engage, ask a lot of questions, and be authentic. It's not up to you to change a boy's heart. Speak his language, whatever it may be, and you just might be able to overcome the language barrier.

SOLID ROCK

Situation:

> Young men are constantly bombarded with worldviews that oppose Scripture.

Mission:

> Help them prepare their minds for critical thinking and mental warfare.

Execution:

★ GIVE THEM CHALLENGE

Dubois, Wyoming is the geographic Middle of Nowhere. It's a little town of about a thousand mountain dwellers who are shirt-off-their-back friendly and view "city folk" with healthy suspicion. I'm not kidding when I say that there's nothing out there.

Trees and mountains are there, and the occasional moose, but that's about it. And it's precisely why we go there every year for summer camp, which we call Solid Rock.

For one week out of the year, we take the youth group kids to a ranch in the mountains for an intensive time of fun, learning, and grizzly bear hunting. Okay, maybe we aren't actually hunting the bears, but all the guys will sharpen branches into spears and we will go "bear hunting."

If we ever actually encountered a bear, I'm sure that these brave warriors would squeal like little girls, but the point is to encourage them to explore their wild side. Whitewater rafting, sleeping under the stars, campfire games, many things go on during that week. It's for all the students, boys and girls, but I believe the guys get the most out of it. The reason? Challenge and danger.

The "challenge" part is the mental exercises that we put them through. The "danger" is the roaring rapids, wandering grizzly bears, and perilous drop-offs. We even have some great sessions held twice a day. You wouldn't think that teenagers from a large city might find it fun to listen two hours a day to a guy drone on about morals and ethics while in the mountains, but they do. Maybe it's because we start out by asking them to explain why murdering a child is wrong.

I meant it exactly like you just read it. The very first topic of the first session at camp involves defending why it would be "wrong" to ruthlessly murder a kindergartener. The next session's topic involves defending why it is "good" to feed a starving orphan. It's safe to say that none of them ever had a youth pastor begin a summer camp with *that* subject.

We don't let them off the hook with any simple answers. If they answer something like, "It's wrong because it is against the law," then we reply with, "It was against the law in Nazi Germany to protect Jews from the concentration camps, so are you certain that 'law' is the best way to determine if something is right or wrong?" Again, dumb looks on faces begin to occur so we lead them on a little bit more. "It's just wrong" is not allowed to be an answer for any of them. No one is cut any slack. Everyone has to explain why murder is wrong and helping needy people is good. This can lead to mass confusion during the first couple of days because all of them demand to know what the answer is. We, the leaders, don't give them the answers yet because we want them to come to their own conclusions first.

You might be thinking that this is an extremely bizarre method of discipleship, and you're exactly right. It *is* bizarre. But what we are trying to do is get them to unclog their MTV-stuffed brains and reason out their own beliefs. Don't give us the religious answer, we tell them, because the religious answer is not always the right answer. If you're going to claim to believe in Jesus Christ, you'd better know why.

What this does is force them to consider the consequences of what they believe. We don't force a lot of Scripture verses into their heads or spend time in theological examination. The Bible is the basis for all that we do, but it's hard to argue for the truth of Scripture with a smart unbelieving person if they can't even answer why murder might be wrong. This is not an effort to reason away the Holy Spirit, as some might claim, but instead become proficient with another weapon in our arsenal—the mind.

I mentioned the postmodern world earlier and the effect that it has on morals. The students eventually figure out on their own, without us telling them, that there must be a God who makes the Rules. We all know the Rules without knowing why, so it must be inside us somewhere to know God. Morally, the senseless killing of a child is awful. Everyone but the completely deranged would agree. Why do you feel the need to call it awful? Because a moral conscience is written into you by God.

We may be covered in wickedness, and in our flesh dwells no good thing, but somewhere deep inside us is the ability to understand right and wrong. Accepting or rejecting that is the dilemma the human race finds itself in.

Okay, fine, that sounds like some exceedingly boring philosophy lecture, I admit. But the reaction of the students is remarkable. They *get* it. Despite a day of exhausting fun miles away from home, they sit still and listen. They start to come to an understanding that there must be a God out there, and if He is out there, how do we come to know more about Him? Bingo, there's the opening. Evangelism Shark alert! (There's nothing wrong with the Evangelism Shark. It's more a matter of how it is used).

As the week goes on the challenge to the kids is simple: know why you believe what you believe. Don't march around preening about how Christian you are. If you believe it, be able to articulate it. I am certainly not saying that they should ignore the testimony of powerful transformation in their lives brought by the Holy Spirit. It's the most powerful evidence we have. They should do that, and also "be ready to give an account" to everyone for their beliefs, as it is commanded in 1 Peter 3:15.

★ LET THEM EXAMINE

The point of this is to emphasize that letting young men ask the deep questions and challenge the assumptions of faith is not a bad thing. You don't need to hide them from ideas that contradict Christianity. If they are never exposed to what the enemy is throwing at them then what kind of training are they doing? Never once in my Army career have I been a part of any training that didn't attempt to simulate actual combat. We can't afford the luxury of pretending the enemy doesn't exist. An army in the barracks has highly polished boots, but the fight ain't in the barracks.

In Acts 19:8 it says that Paul argued and persuaded people concerning the Kingdom of God. Obviously there must be something to this notion of persuasion or else Paul, the greatest missionary our faith has ever known and human author of 2 / 3 of the New Testament, wouldn't have wasted time with it. By doing this he demonstrated that it was good to develop the mind for battle so that the Gospel could be spread more effectively to all mankind. Knowing Jesus doesn't mean you have to commit intellectual suicide.

Jesus would ask his disciples very penetrating questions designed to challenge them. On one occasion He asked them, "Who do the people say that I am?" (Luke 9:18). They replied that some said he was another John the Baptist, others claimed he was like one of the prophets of old. He then asked them, "But who do you say that I am?" (Luke 9:20).

There are two points that it appears Jesus is trying to make to His disciples. The first is that He wants to test them in their knowledge of beliefs the people have. It would do the disciples no good if they sat around debating theology in their own little world while the masses of people were ignored. It's irresponsible of us to close our ears like children and scream, "Blah, blah, blah! Can't hear you! Blah, blah, blah!"

There isn't a passage anywhere in the Bible that tells Christians to isolate themselves. We may not like what the culture is throwing at us, and I am not saying we should say or do anything morally compromising, but we *are* supposed to be all things to all men, according to 1 Corinthians 9:22. Taken with the actions of Paul in Acts 17, the evidence seems to indicate that rather than merely ignoring the influences of the world, we need to be actively learning about who people say Jesus is. We should be shining our lights, in other words.

The second question Jesus asks the disciples is who *they* say He is. Allow me to translate this into teenage language: "All right dude, that's all good that you can tell me who others are saying I am. But do *you* really know who I am?"

Peter, as usual, was quick with an answer, but I think the silence of the other apostles is remarkable. That question must have really penetrated their hearts. I can picture them looking around at each other, thinking, "Well, who do I think this guy is? I left everything to follow Him, and so did these other men, but do I really know who He is?"

It is this topic that provides the basis for Solid Rock camp: establishing the firm foundation of belief that will allow them to withstand the assault of ideas outside the safety of your home. Laying such foundations with boys will help them to think clearly when challenges come. I'm not saying you should shop around for youth groups that do Solid Rock-like camps, but do try to expose them to influences that will challenge their faith.

The most difficult teenage boys to speak with about things related to Christianity are the kids who have grown up in church, attend Christian academies, or are home schooled in a rigorously religious environment. Boys who come from dysfunctional homes or from the streets are refreshingly honest about their beliefs and it's pretty easy to slide into a conversation with them. Lifelong church kids are tougher eggs to crack. The reason for this is they've learned very early and very well the language of Christians and the culture of church. They can say exactly what you want to hear and completely fool you into believing they are right with God.

Of all the boys who worry me the most, it's these guys who seem to have it all together. If a parent tells me how much of a leader their son was in his previous youth group and I notice that he is arrogant with his answers in Sunday School, I'll worry about that kid much sooner than the atheist Gangster who may walk in. I do this because I *was* one of these guys.

Growing up in a pastor's house, I could speak the language and quote all of the necessary verses in order to make myself look good to the religious people. My folks never once pressured me into it, but looking good in front of people is no less a temptation in church than any other place.

I loved being the guy that knew the answer. Whenever the youth pastor would ask the group a question I wanted to be the one who could dazzle the group with my Scriptural know-how. It was arrogance, pure and simple. I knew Jesus, but I didn't *know* Jesus.

The day it finally came crashing down on me was during my senior year of high school. I had befriended a large number of Mormon classmates and loved to spar with them about spiritual matters. All of the kids in my youth group looked to me in order to handle the tough questions, because the Latter Day Saints church does a much better job of preparing their youngsters for the clash of worldviews.

A buddy of mine finally invited me to come to his house

in order to meet with some Mormon missionaries. I was thrilled. Finally, a chance to show off how smart I was! The day was set, and about ten of us showed up at my friend's house to meet these missionaries. They were pretty stunned that so many Bible-wielding teenagers with bloodlust in their eyes had bothered to come.

I was the Alpha Male of this group of Soldiers for Jesus (according to us). I'm certain that God was laughing to Himself as He watched our spiritual pride cram into that living room with pens and papers poised for action. The first session with the missionaries went really well because they had no answer for our carefully researched arguments. I took great care to make them *think* I was interested in what they had to say, when in reality I was just circling like the Evangelism Shark.

We left them with the promise to gather again the following week. They said they had someone they wanted me to meet so I was even more excited. *They need to bring in their big guns to deal with me*, I remember thinking. Then I reminded myself to not be so arrogant with my superior debating skills. Did you catch that? *Remind* myself.

The next week's meeting was packed out once more, but this time there was a new face among the missionaries. A younger guy with sandy blonde hair and an engaging smile. I liked him right away, but I smelled blood in the water. The Shark was about to attack once again. Then he started to speak to us, and my entire life blew up.

He spoke about how he was a Christian like we were, had gone to seminary and become a pastor. He talked about the authenticity of a walk with Jesus, and how false religion was unnecessary. He reasoned with us very gently from the Scriptures, quoting verse after verse and making a multitude of theologically profound arguments. He culminated his talk with an emotionally wrenching description of how he came to see mainline protestant denominations as empty and that true joy was only found in the Latter Day Saints church. The real Jesus was revealed in the Mormon scriptures, he said, and his conversion to Mormonism was the turning point of his life. His first conversion had been a false one, and now he was on the right track.

It was completely spellbinding. There was nothing I could say. Nothing. No smart aleck remark, no brilliantly incisive comment. I had gotten my clock cleaned, torn apart, and then dashed on the rocks. My friends all looked at me for the answers I was sure to have, but I could only babble on stupidly.

The Dallas Cowboys once beat the Buffalo Bills 52–17 in the Superbowl. I felt like the Bills head coach at that moment. As an Army buddy once put it, "Some days you're the dog, and some days you're the fire hydrant." Leaving that house was the first step in my struggle of quiet desperation with God. My happy little world where I was always right had been crushed, and now I didn't even know what I believed anymore. Which Jesus was real? That guy had been so convincing, his testimony so emotionally wrenching that I honestly believe only the wisest of Christians could have resisted it.

It was a long journey for me, and a subtle one. My parents didn't know about it, neither did my church friends. There was an image to maintain. No one could know about the turmoil because then I would stop being Answer Guy. So I began my search for the real Jesus. It took several years and many dark hours of soul searching. I read the claims of Mormonism, studied the Bible, and investigated everything I could get my hands on that dealt with the Mormon religion. The Lord allowed me to go through that process, and there was never any specific moment that it ended, but I finally came to understand that Jesus, with all the religion stripped away, is Who He said He was. I eventually trusted the Bible as the only authoritative source for who God was, because I saw with a mind full of evidence and a heart full of faith. I came to not only know Him, but as Paul put it in Philippians 3:10, to know the *power* of His resurrection.

What did it? I don't know. But I learned that spiritual growth is a long journey, sometimes agonizingly so. There are no quick fixes. Quoting a verse or knowing the Apostle's Creed by heart does nothing to heal a wounded spirit. I was raised as nearly perfectly as a boy can be raised, in a pastor's home with loving parents, and I still suffered this near-defeat.

Be gentle with your son; let him work out his own salvation, like it says in Philippians 2:12, with fear and trembling. He needs to wrestle with God some before he will hear the call of duty. The outpouring testimony of a changed heart is the most critical piece of evidence that we have, but it is false to assume that it excuses us from ever developing our minds. Peter and Paul were both pretty adamant about defending the faith skillfully.

We need to be ready to offer a well-articulated response when people ask why we are Christians. I wasn't ready and I got burned. Likewise, you can know all the facts, but there's no power in it without the power of the Spirit.

Postmodern teenagers live in a world of emotional experience. It's where the whole "what's true for you is fine as long as you don't offend me" mentality came from. So I would suggest that challenging their minds is one place to start when dealing with lifelong churchgoers. Guys love a challenge. Doing something as simple as discussing why things are good or evil can be a good starting point.

With the churchgoing teen, be aware of him fooling everyone with his spiritual success. If things are going a little *too* well, like nothing ever seems to bug him or he never has any problem with spiritual matters, then challenge him. Don't make him memorize even more Scripture; maybe instead ask some questions of him. "What do you believe, son?"

Ask it in such a way that he won't think you're dogging him, but that you honestly want to know. If the answer sounds fake, just say something like, "Come on, be real with me, you don't need to give me a religious answer." The language you use is the most important part of this process. Don't bombard him with scary spiritual words; just talk to him.

Boys, no matter the category, love a challenge. It's built into them. Their minds are no exception. Like Paul in Athens, showing even a basic understanding of the beliefs of a young person can go a long way. Asking questions first, instead of giving answers, demonstrates that you have respect for their opinion. It may be a completely wrong opinion but that shouldn't prevent you from learning it.

Their world is much more complex than yours was due to the formation of one phenomenon: the internet. The internet, regardless of how much they have been sheltered, will continue to bring new ideas and issues into the lives of teen guys at a much higher rate than ever before.

With every click on a new website, information that would have taken previous generations many years of life experience to accumulate is now instantly deposited into a young mind. They aren't always ready to handle it and are forced to mature at ever-increasing rates. That, combined with the biological and emotional confusion that teens have *always* experienced, makes for one big mess.

Let them wrestle, let them probe, let them examine, let them seek. Jesus promises rest to those who are weary. Boys need to feel weary before they will seek Jesus, and we can't force them into it. It has to be *their* relationship with the Savior, not ours.

WARRIORS NEEDED

The Lord is a warrior; The Lord is His name.

Exodus 15:3

I have nothing to offer but blood, toil, tears and sweat. ... You ask, what is our policy? I say it is to wage war by land, sea, and air. War with all our might and with all the strength God has given us, and to wage war against a monstrous tyranny never surpassed in the dark and lamentable catalogue of human crime. That is our policy.

Winston Churchill

Situation:

Men are abandoning their positions as husbands and fathers. Families are suffering. The next generation is heading the same direction. Boys see a relationship with Christ as boring and it is causing them to abandon the faith. Immediate action required.

Mission:

Train the next generation of young men to become warriors. Call them to service in a cause greater than themselves. Help them understand the difference between religion and Jesus.

Execution:

★ DESTROY THE MYTH THAT
CHRISTIANITY IS FOR WIMPS

There is a giant sword hanging on the wall of my office. I look up at it every single time I walk in and remember what my life is supposed to be: a constant, unrelenting war for the Kingdom of God. Before someone panics and assumes I am trying to start a jihad, let me clarify that this war is completely in the spiritual realm. The weapons are not physical, but according to 2 Corinthians 2:4 they *are* for the destruction of evil fortresses. It's worth pointing out the whole evil fortress thing to your son so that he knows they don't just exist in video games.

The sword was given to me by a fellow soldier the night before I got married. A bunch of us were gathered around a campfire in the woods for a "bachelor party" where some of my friends could speak words of wisdom into my life. He asked that everyone remain silent for a moment and, reaching behind a tree nearby, produced the sword. In a very serious tone he began to list all of the things that would be required of me as the man in my household and as a husband and father. The sword, he told me, was to remind me every day of my life to never fall asleep on the battlefield.

I falter and fall asleep on the battlefield once in a while, just like every other guy. But the sword reminds me to shake off the dirt, get back on the horse, and charge once again. I take that sword with me whenever I teach at the church or speak at a school. It catches everyone's attention immediately. Something about it makes the boys in the room clench their jaws and stiffen their backbones.

The view of many young men is that Jesus must be a wimp. They hate coming to church and are bored silly in the service because they think that everything about Jesus involves cuddling lambs and weeping about problems. Basically, that church is only for women. Can we honestly blame them? It gets frustrating to see all these portrayals of Jesus as a feminine figure with delicate features.

The love, mercy, and grace of God are life-changing, so the problem isn't with presenting that side of Him. The problem is presenting *only* that side of Him. There are a bunch of flat out awesome stories in the Bible. Not just the famous ones like Noah's Ark or the Ten Commandments. I'm talking about the manly war stories that outdo anything Hollywood has ever come up with. David and the Mighty Men get entire chapters devoted to nothing but their heroic deeds.

One dude named Benaiah climbed down into a pit and killed a lion. The best part? Scripture says that it was snowing. I love that. There's no reason to describe the scene in such graphic detail other than the fact that it's *manly*. Killing lions in a pit on a snowy day? That beats any action movie ever made. Josheb-bashebeth, the chief of the Mighty Men, brought down 800 men in one day with only his spear. 800 to 1 odds? Psh. That's nothing if you're one of the Mighty Men.

It never fails. The stories about war, courage, and valor capture their attention immediately. The verses about love and mercy put them right to sleep. Literally. I've had to throw a few objects at snoozing Knuckleheads while speaking about 1 John.

The second I mention something that involves conflict or battle, though, every male in the room sits a little taller in his chair and listens up. There's something about the nature of war that drives a boy's heartbeat. From early in childhood when they play with little green Army men or run around bashing things with the remote control, conflict is sought. My one year-old devotes himself to finding new ways to demolish our bookshelf. A Christmas tree provides too much temptation for him to bear.

I mentioned a boy's love of conflict earlier, so here's how it relates to Christianity. Rather than tame down boys and force them to listen to how much love and grace flows, we should be setting the fires of war inside them. They should be hearing the call of duty that Jesus provides. Being a man requires taking the hard road and doing the hard thing, at all times and at all costs. At no point is a man to sit back and rest on the laurels of his success. This notion of retirement from doing anything but playing golf is a Western cultural lie, and it feeds the false identity that men have accepted. Looking for the easy road and being passive is what leads men to abandon their families. Boys pick up on it and do the very same thing their father did. "The wife and kids cramp my style, so I'm outta here."

Caleb, when Joshua was dividing the Promised Land among the tribes after the conquest, demanded to be given the country where the giants were. He didn't want the beach-front property as his inheritance. No sir, he looked Joshua straight in the eye and demanded the roughest terrain available, because *that* was where the fight was.

The best part? Caleb was in his eighties. Joshua 14:12, in my own words, reads something like this: "*Don't you even think about giving me the golf resort area, Joshua. I'm just as* strong as I ever was. This gray hair is only the sign of how tough I am. Give me the country that will demand the most out of me! Give me the violence, I'm not afraid of it!"* (Paraphrase).

You're only allowed to stop fighting when you're dead, as the Marines like to say.

I am not glorifying physical war and demanding that we go looking for it. If your son grows up and starts a war with some obscure country, don't come blaming me. What I'm saying is that God designed a man with conflict in mind. He ordered Adam to "subdue the earth." Well, that involves conflict, since after Adam messed up, God also promised in Genesis 3 that nothing would ever come easily for the man.

Boys live lives of spiritual desperation, searching for the song that will finally command them. They need to feel called to a greater duty, an unrelenting battle that will demand absolute commitment even to death. As OSG J.I. Packer once put it, we need to have a big enough objective that lays hold of our allegiance. Doing wicked things will lose their appeal when a boy sees that his portion of the battlefield exists for him to fill it. God designed him with war in mind, and He's carved out a niche in the fight for him to fit

★TEACH HIM THE WAY OF THE WARRIOR.

Ryan wasn't enjoying the boys retreat. True, it was out in the middle of a ranch in south Texas, where only those that can appreciate it actually appreciate it. Snakes, scorpions, spiders, and mountain lions roam free down there. City kids usually require a period of adjustment. The other guys were shooting things with .22 rifles and trying to catch bullfrogs the size of chickens, but Ryan kept mostly to himself. He would plug his earphones in and tune out the rest of us.

My policy is to get them to *want* to remove their earphones. If I just make them do it because I said so, then all they're doing is counting down the time until they can put them back in again. Provide an alternative, though, and they'll usually turn the iPod off on their own.

I had made it my mission for the weekend to get Ryan to do something that scared the living daylights out of him, and I was going to do it using Old Hoss. This wasn't the original Old Hoss. That Ford truck had gone on to its reward in Hunting Rig Heaven. This was Hoss Junior, but out of nostalgia, we at the hunting camp still called it Old Hoss.

For those not familiar with how hunting is done down in south Texas, the first sight of our camouflaged trucks with deer blind towers built onto the back driving down the highway might remind you of *Deliverance*. Sure it's goofy, but guys love it. The boys were having a blast just sitting on top of the 15-foot rig and driving down the back roads kicking up dust.

Ryan was having none of it. Heights were a major problem for him and he kept sitting on the tailgate looking like he would rather be anywhere in the world than where he was at that moment. I could tell he was embarrassed because he thought the other guys saw him as a coward.

I sat down at dinner with him the first evening and told him that you're only brave if you are scared of what you're doing. If you aren't scared of it and you do it, you're not brave. That's the whole point of bravery, doing something even when it scares you. So those other kids careening carelessly on the top of the hunting rig, I told him, weren't proving their bravery because they weren't afraid of it.

For the first time he looked interested in what I had to say. "That kinda makes sense, I guess."

"Yeah, bro, you don't need to ride up top if you don't want to, but I'm telling ya, I think you'd enjoy it. Be a great way to test how brave you are. You'll never know 'til you know," I replied.

As the weekend unfolded, slowly but surely I was able to persuade him to get on top of the rig. He started out lying prostrate on the floor and then worked his way up to a sitting position, then kneeling, and finally, on the last ride of the weekend, he stood tall and felt the wind in his face and screamed his head off as we sailed through the desert. There was a warrior buried somewhere in between those headphones. He just needed to be shown the way.

Basic Combat Training is not fun. It isn't supposed to be. I've done harder things in my military career, but there was something about that first introduction to Army life that really got under my skin. Independent personalities like mine are not welcome. Scratch that—they're welcome in the way that a cat welcomes a mouse to a cheese party.

I walked in the day after September 11 and signed my life away to service. Some will tell you that we only do it for the enlistment bonus or because we're desperately needy. Don't listen to 'em. It was one of the best decisions I've made yet. I tell the young men I speak to that it isn't for everyone and they have to really feel called to it, but if they do then it's an experience unlike any other. Nothing better for warrior training than actual warrior training.

The recruiters are really nice and tell you to call them by their first names. They even give you a can of soda and wax eloquently about how wonderful life in the service is. For a couple of weeks you're proud of yourself for stepping forward and have talked yourself into believing that it's as fun as the commercials make it out to be. Wizened old veterans chuckle when you tell them about how "the Army is different now" and pat you on the back. This causes a marked increase in the level of nervousness you experience shortly before shipping out. Your family cries a lot and you try to look noble, promising them that you'll be fine and that you alone are needed to save the world from terrorists.

Arriving at the fort for basic combat training, any semblance of your individualism and unique-snowflakeness is smashed like a spider under a combat boot. They shave your head and issue you some hideous glasses that look like a preschool craft project (which I had experience with, by the way). These glasses have gone by a variety of affectionate nicknames in days of yore, with my personal favorite being BCG's (Birth Control Glasses). They received that name because it is a mathematical impossibility that immoralities between male and female soldiers can occur when wearing them. No one finds you attractive if you look like a Muppet, not even after five months of quarantine in a barracks. The purpose of these ghastly objects is to finish off the last of your pride. Everyone looks exactly alike, with shaved heads and huge red spectacles.

The goal is to produce teamwork. You are now part of

a Team. No longer do you think and function individually, although that is allowed to return upon the completion of initial training.

You're forced onto cattle cars and told to moo loudly while being transported to your barracks. I'm not sure why it is that "mooing" works for so many things, but there must be something to it. The first day, and every day after that, is a blur of mud, pushups, and screaming. Some people don't have any problem with this, but for those of us who are highly individualistic and don't like being told what to do, following your bunkmate into the bathroom stall in order to develop Teamwork is … well, let's just say you would prefer a group hug. Worst of all, we had to dig an enormous ditch on Super Bowl Sunday when it was eight degrees below zero while the drill sergeants watched the game inside.

You have to cram with fifty other guys into one shower stall and only have thirty seconds to bathe yourself. They count it down, too. After the speed shower, you get another whole ten seconds to put on a physical fitness uniform. Running back out into the bay, you are blessed with an additional hour of physical training and sweating and rolling in the mud, thus doing away with the whole purpose of showering. Imagine this exact process every night for five months. I've heard that basic training is easier now and that's a shame. Of course, I say that from the comfort of my chair with those days long behind me. Some poor Muppet-looking fellow at a fort somewhere is digging ditches in subzero weather.

In the middle of all this, there was one drill sergeant who screamed the loudest and was everywhere at once. *Anything* we did was seen by this guy. Every false step, every short-cut we tried to take was spotted. He would knock over our clothing lockers and throw our mattresses out the window. He'd run through the bay shaking baking soda everywhere and tell us it was snowing and we'd better get the plows out. He made us turn our cups over and over in the dining hall throughout the thirty seconds allotted for eating. He was a relentless irritant. The floor was cleaned so well overnight that hospital patients could have safely eaten off of it, and he would still tell us it looked like a swamp. I hated everything about him—until I realized what he was up to.

He was molding us into warriors. He didn't care about our feelings getting hurt or the boo-boos on our knees. He declared in no uncertain terms that by the time he was done with us, there wouldn't be a soft bone left in our bodies. Even scrubbing the bathroom four hours every night was purging us of sissiness. What we didn't realize at the time was that he was preparing us for combat, a nasty event that makes no sense and weeds out the weak from the strong. The more you bleed in training, he would say, the less you will bleed in war.

His name was Drill Sergeant McCall, and he was a warrior. The moment I realized it was at Warrior Tower, a giant climbing wall where the Army decides to remove any fear of heights that you may have. I had no problem with it but the guy behind me was frozen with fear. No matter how much screaming and prodding Drill Sergeant McCall would do, this kid did not want to climb that tower.

We all watched the instructor to see what he would do with the soldier. Some of us, feeling brave again, made clucking noises. McCall suddenly turned on us with all his rage and made us do pushups in the Hog Waller (a pit of muddy water that served as a disciplinarian) till our arms fell off. "Nobody," he screamed in our ears, "will *ever* call their battle buddy a chicken again! I *promise* I will make you *want to die* from the pushups you will do if I ever hear that again!"

While we were wishing for death in the Hog Waller I happened to catch a glimpse of McCallin walking back towards the soldier frozen on the tower. Instead of resuming his tirade, he effortlessly climbed the 20 feet up a cargo net until he was level with the kid. In a gentle voice, he started coaching him. Persuading him. Encouraging him. Affirming him. Calling him to duty. Slowly the young man looked up, wiped the sweat from his forehead, and kept moving up the wall. Each step he gained there was a little more encouragement from the instructor. Reaching the top, the young man threw up his arms and gave a war-whoop of triumph, and I saw Drill Sergeant McCall clap him on the back and beam like a proud father.

That was a vivid, powerful, striking glimpse of God: dreadful when he was purging our weaknesses, and gentle when all hope seemed lost. There are times when we need the firm discipline of the Father, but there are others where the warm embrace of Jesus restores our spirit in full.

The rest of our training until graduation day we revered him. If he walked through the bay screaming, we rushed to do the job well not out of fear, but out of desire to please him. He could have grabbed me by the shoulder and said, "Graham, here's a bucket of gasoline, I want you to go into that burning building and douse the flames with it," and I would have done it. I have no idea if Drill Sergeant McCall was a Christian or not. I only know that a young man who had been paralyzed with terror and uncertainty was able to scale Warrior Tower because he was led by a *warrior*. By the end of the five months he had become the most admired and beloved person in our world. Be that kind of leader, fathers, and your sons will follow you anywhere.

A fantastic way to explain what God requires of a young man is to tell him that he needs to live like a warrior. How does he do that?

In Psalm 15, King David ponders what is required of the man who wants to ascend the mountain of God:

> He who walks with integrity, and works righteousness, and speaks truth in his heart. He does not slander with his tongue, nor does evil to his neighbor, nor takes up a reproach to his friend; in whose eyes a reprobate is despised, but who honors those who fear the Lord; He swears to his own hurt … (Psalm 15).

Long before the Code of Chivalry existed this passage of Scripture was calling men to greater service. In fact some have argued that the code was inspired by it. My father read this passage to me when I was 17 and we were on a safari in Africa (it was my senior present, a lifelong dream of ours). I will never, until my dying breath, forget sitting in that little mud safari hut and listening to him read it to me with the passion and conviction so characteristic of him. It wasn't, "Son, here are the rules, obey them or you are going to fail." It was more along the lines of, "Son, this is what it takes. You have it. Go for it."

It should be a humbling experience to think about ascending the mountain of God. Tread not lightly upon it, in other words. The man who wants to do so must live by a higher standard of devotion and excellence. His strength comes from the Lord, but he must have the courage to be fully obedient to Christ. Instead of just listing the do's and don'ts of Psalm 15, try framing it like this: "Think you're tough? Walk with integrity. Keep your promises. Stand against evil. Do that, and *then* you will be tough." That sort of thing is much more inspiring to a young man lacking direction than wishy-washy sentiments and group hugs. No battlefield commander I ever read about scheduled self-esteem meetings in the moments leading up to the battle.

It pains me greatly to admit it, but the Marine Corps has a much better recruiting program than the Army. While the Army was wasting a lot of years begging and pleading people to join, the Marines advertised themselves like this: "We're bad dudes. Don't mess with us. You think you have what it takes? Then come and find out, but don't go crying to mama if you can't hack it." They air commercials which have a lot of imagery about fighting dragons and wielding swords.

The Army, meanwhile, still can't seem to get the hint that pictures of cute little blonde female soldiers smiling with self-esteem smiles don't activate any warrior mechanisms in a man. Guys don't want to hear only about the college money you can get. They want to become part of an elite brotherhood that lives with maximum force at all times. Female soldiers are welcome, but the majority of warriors are men. It's how they're designed. Regardless of what efforts the agents of political correctness expend, men will always make up the majority of armies. The results of this advertising are telling:

The Army struggles to make its quota every year, and the Marines have no problem filling their ranks.

Let's examine the Code of Chivalry a little further and see if there's anything useful to be found in it. Some say the Code is outdated and chauvinistic, but maybe it's exactly what we need.

★ LOVE THE LORD

The compassion of Jesus will appeal to boys when they've reached a level of maturity in their walk or they come to a place of desperate need. Until then, "the Lord is a warrior" is usually more exciting than "Jesus wept."

Don't automatically think that because a boy doesn't mention the word "heart" a lot when talking about Jesus that he doesn't have spiritual tenderness. It just needs to be rough-sounding for him to understand it. When the Lord was giving commands to Joshua at the beginning of the conquest, He won Joshua's undying loyalty with a speech that's a high point of Scriptural manliness:

> Every place the sole of your foot treads, I have given it to you, just as I spoke to Moses. From the wilderness and this Lebanon, even as far as the great river, the river Euphrates, all the land of the Hittites, and as far as the Great Sea toward the setting of the sun, will be your territory. *No man will be able to stand before you all the days of your life.* Just as I have been with Moses, I will be with you; I will not fail you or forsake you. Be strong and courageous, for you shall give this people possession of the land which I swore to their fathers to give them... have I not commanded you? Be strong and courageous! Do not tremble or be dismayed, for the Lord your God is with you wherever you go. Joshua 1:5–7

Now *that* makes you sit forward and pay attention. Joshua

would have a lifetime of continuous victory if He followed the Lord's commandments. When he finally died he received a simple title: the servant of the Lord. A man can ask for no higher honor than that.

God doesn't promise us safety and we aren't the ones who declare victory. He just says, "Look, be a man and listen up. It's gonna be hard and you need to be strong, but do exactly what I say and you'll get through it all right." He doesn't describe how to be strong. He says to follow His commands, but being strong is something he created in every man. We only need to obey the instinct. There's a reason that God always told the men of the Bible to gird their loins like men. He never told it to the women, not once. That doesn't mean that women can't be strong, but the very word *strong* should be so ingrained in a man that merely saying it makes him leap to action.

We loved Drill Sergeant McCall because he inspired us to greatness. But unlike Drill Sergeant McCall, Jesus doesn't approve of us based mainly upon our performance. Boys will eventually learn that, but we have to trust God's timing. That will come, don't worry. They'll be bawling like babies when they feel the full force of conviction hit them. For starters, give 'em a call to arms when you are telling them about Jesus.

★ HONOR THE LADIES

The media culture has relegated women to the status of pieces of flesh that exist to sexually gratify men. This particular little lie can demolish a girl's view of herself and value before God. Teaching your boy that the girl being rapped about in the hip hop song is someone's sister or daughter may help him think twice.

It's tough, because the modern culture tells girls to be heartlessly self-reliant. That's positive because girls should pursue their individual calling freely, but it can also turn them into man-haters. A boy may open the door for a girl and then receive a lecture about how only knuckle-dragging cavemen open doors for women, and she can open her *own* door, thank you very much. To which you can say, "Great job and keep doing it, son. It doesn't matter if you ever get a single compliment for it. You're one more man willing to stand for honor."

I was wasting some time not long ago watching the season finale of a television show called *The Bachelor*. I've always been intrigued by the amount of work people will invest in something so stupid. The show is about a guy, picked by the television network, who gets a chance to woo dozens of women, also picked by the television network. The "story" of the show is to see if any of the lovely ladies can be the one he chooses to romance. He kisses all of these women at one time, and the suspense is which one he will choose at the end of the show.

My wife Cassandra and I were stunned at how gullible these girls were. The dude was living out every man's twisted fantasy by having multiple beautiful women at one time vie to be with him with the full knowledge of one another. The high ratings for the show indicate that the public is buying into this. Surprised I would watch such drivel? It's a fascinating glimpse into the state of our culture, and you have to go searching for illustrations sometimes anyway.

The commentary on our culture's depravity aside, the episode that I watched was a shocker: The guy ended up not picking *any* of the girls. Horrors! The live studio audience (full of women) harpooned this guy for an hour, with question after question about why he didn't love so-and-so. I was chuckling at the man's self-inflicted dilemma when he said something that totally caught me off guard. When asked to explain himself, he replied, clearly distraught, that "I didn't *love* any of them. I didn't want to lead any of them on and make them think that I did."

I was intrigued by this and told my wife that we just witnessed one of the most remarkable displays of integrity in television reality show history. She told me that she had half a mind to call the San Antonio Mental Health services and report a madman in her home. I then presented my argument, which was that despite the questionable aspects of his character which would lead him to appear on such a wasteland of a program, the guy still did the right thing.

It hurt, it was embarrassing, he was reviled by the millions watching in their living rooms, but somewhere deep in his masculine soul the voice of nobility called him to duty and he responded. He could have given in to the urge of his flesh. He could have fallen asleep on the battlefield. Instead, the DNA of his authentic manhood whispered a single phrase to his heart: *Honor the Ladies.*

Guys experience physical urges that women will never fully understand. It's incredibly hard to think noble thoughts when you're a teenager with raging hormones, so affirming a boy who is trying can do wonders. If your son is struggling with pornography, it's important to understand that he's no different than every other man that has ever lived. It will never go away. Steve Arterburn wrote a book called *Every Man's Battle* which correctly asserts that regardless of whether a guy is married or not, lust could always be a struggle. Your role as parents ought to be preventing his access to it at home and then trying to help him understand the horrors of it. Forced prostitution in Asia, or minor girls lying about their age in order to star in pornographic films, or the fact that it is someone's sister or daughter in that picture are effective conversation starters about the dangers of dirty internet sites. That won't curb his lustful feelings, but it will give him something to think about.

His desire to look at porn is driven by the male fleshly sin in his heart, and only the Holy Spirit can convict a heart. Rest in the truth that Christ hasn't forgotten about you and will move in your son's heart in His good time. Any guy that treats a girl with respect is bucking modern societal norms and must be commended for it. Teach them that it is through the power and strength of Christ alone that they can overcome. Whether they listen to you or not, remember that the Spirit is in control. Tapping His power is the only way to win the fight, but it's a crawl, not a sprint. Please be patient and just continue drenching him in prayer.

★ DEFEND THE WEAK

Our men's ministry has a motto: *Droit Et Avant.* "Know the right, and do it." Physical combat isn't the main way that a boy should try to become a warrior. Many great battle-field heroes were complete cowards in their personal lives.

A young man taught that character determines what kind of man he will become is more likely to withstand assault.

William Wilberforce was one of the greatest heroes of his time and never spent a minute in a soldier's uniform. He was a member of the British parliament in the 18th century who made it his life goal to see the end of the slave trade. Wilberforce waged his wars in the meeting rooms and corridors of colonial power, reasoning and persuading and never giving up. After years of struggle, he finally got a bill passed, displaying a level of heroics that never needed to be tested on a battlefield. He was a warrior of compassion.

I have a brother-in-law who wages war in fields of compassion. I didn't understand at first why he was so driven. It wasn't that I didn't think we needed to help starving children or war refugees, I just never understood what drove him so hard to it. Then I realized that it was his warrior soul being channeled in a different direction than mine. When he sees the plight of the desperate, he feels the same rush of courage and sacrifice that I would feel if a criminal were attacking an old woman. It's equally heroic, equally masculine, and equally Scriptural. His wife is just as dedicated as he is. Since mercy and compassion are usually thought of as "women's work," it's marvelous to see a young man completely sold-out to the cause of mercy to the glory of Christ.

So waging a good war doesn't imply physical combat … but it's still fun to test the fighting part out. Whenever I speak at a chapel service or school, in addition to bringing a sword along, I spend the first part of the time I have teaching them hand-to-hand combat skills. Some parents have been flustered asunder by this, but the overwhelming response is positive. I'm careful to remind them that you don't try this out on your little brother or sister (however tempting it may be) but you should see the flame igniting in their eyes when they're learning actual battlefield skills. Most of those boys will never spend one second of their life in a struggle to the death...but they *will* feel like they're prepared if the day ever comes to defend the weak.

A boy can be obedient to God's call of duty even on a playground. Those that are helpless need a boy with a warrior's heart to protect them from harm, even if body blows never get exchanged. There's a Charlie Brown special titled *He's a Bully, Charlie Brown* that illustrates this well. Charlie Brown and the gang are at summer camp and a boy starts to bully the younger kids while playing marbles. He's shooting marbles with them and is taking advantage of their inexperience to take their marbles. The complaints against the bully come to Charlie Brown's attention and he investigates the story.

Charlie Brown, the definitive Melting Pot, sees one of his younger friends get taken advantage of and decides he's had enough. Snoopy helps him practice his marble shooting and Charlie finally challenges the bully to a match, winner takes all. It's a close one but Charlie defeats the bully with a well placed final shot. There are cheers and the bully gives the marbles back. No physical conflict took place, but Charlie Brown became a warrior that day. I don't recommend you force your son to watch Charlie Brown specials, but the concept is valid.

A Melting Pot kind of kid may not have a physically imposing body, but that doesn't excuse him from the war. He has a place on the front lines just like every other man.

There's *something* he can fight for in order to defend the weak. Help him find it. There's always another kid who'll need assistance, there will always be a bully to stand up to.

In Proverbs it says to, "Open your mouth, judge righteously, and defend the rights of the afflicted and the needy" (Proverbs 31:9).

Isaiah commands us with, "Learn to do good; seek justice, reprove the ruthless, defend the orphan, plead for the widow" (Isaiah 1:17).

Those are verses calling on all the men of society to take action. Fistfights don't need to take place. Just don't sit around complaining about how bad things are, *do something!* Be a man. If you're not Hercules, don't worry about it. The Lord is with you if you are seeking Him. It ain't the size of the dog in the fight; it's the size of the fight in the dog. When King David was a shepherd boy he tore apart a bear and a lion with just his hands. There wasn't anything exceptional about his physical appearance; he merely let the Spirit of the Lord take over in his time of need.

Dad always told me never to get into fights at school unless it was to protect someone from harm. If that happened, my instructions were clear: I'd better win it. The other kid being bigger and stronger than me was no excuse. It didn't bother David when that Goliath fellow started shooting his mouth off. Being outnumbered and surrounded was merely an annoyance to the Mighty Men.

Last stands are hugely popular among boys. There was a movie released in recent years called 300, and it told the story of the ancient Battle of Thermopylae. I had been eagerly awaiting it, because the true story of a small band of Spartan warriors holding off the invading millions of the Persian Empire is the kind of thing guys love. Unfortunately, the film itself is full of morally bankrupt content and looks more like a music video than an actual movie, but the popularity of it among young men was remarkable. After years of being served wishy-washy heroes and ambiguous messages, a film about heroic men fighting to the death for a great cause resonated strongly among Millenials. As I told our guys, it was disappointing that the message had to come in a movie so bogged down with unnecessarily explicit scenes, but it certainly spoke to a need.

General Chesty Puller during the Korean War said a lot of memorable things, but my personal favorite was his response when told that eight divisions of Chinese soldiers had his men surrounded. "All right, they're on our left, they're on our right, they're in front of us and they're behind us ... they can't get away this time." Long odds are where we should thrive. God is the God of long odds. He never allowed the Israelites to vastly outnumber their opponents because He knew they would begin to think they didn't need Him anymore. To have spent oneself in a worthy cause, or as the Jocks would say it, to "leave it all on the field" is the ultimate satisfaction for men. Boys are no different. The victory is in the fight, not just the outcome. Teen guys will watch something like 300 and long for a chance to prove they have what it takes to be a warrior.

If you're a mom, none of this may be making any sense to you. Nor should it, any more than you and your friends weeping and passing Kleenex boxes around makes sense to your son. One mom found me after church and asked me to help her calm her son down. When I asked her why, she told me it was because she was afraid he wasn't listening to God. I told her, as gently as possible, that the boy wasn't rowdy enough and she should be looking for chances to let him be violent. She probably reported me to the elders, but I stand by it. Passive is much worse than aggressive. So please understand that he's wired differently than you are and needs to hear something you might not find relevant.

★ LET HIM FIND HIS OWN WARRIOR PATH

So we can see why a young man needs to hear the call of duty. What should you do from here? The first and most important task is to drench him in prayer. Pray without ceasing that God would move mightily in his heart. Then wait for Him. It might be an immediate answer to prayer, or it might never happen in your lifetime. The man known as St. Augustine had a mother named Monica who would pray for him night and day. He was a carousing man before coming to Christ, and she never failed to lift him up in prayer. Obviously, it worked. But be content to let God do His thing in His way on His timetable. You can't force change to come to a boy. You also need to be prepared to accept that it isn't up to you to make sure he's right with God.

That said, here's a few ideas:

★ THE JOCK

For a Jock it could be telling him to strive for excellence on the field. Winning isn't the most important part (though it is important). Giving maximum effort at all times and "leaving it all on the field" is. Tell him that he can influence those around him by his determination to glorify God through his physical efforts. It's not about him; it's about God. A great coach can have a tremendous impact in this area; a bad coach can be a good way to teach him lessons about authority.

His struggle will always be the fact that other guys want to be just like him, so his ego will tend to be fat. Girls will probably throw themselves at him with abandon. He's going to need to be strong to resist the hundreds of temptations he'll face each week that other boys less popular don't. This is why it's so vital to encourage nobility and virtue in him, using language that calls forth his inner warrior. He needs to be told that God wants him to not just be a Christian, but be a strong Christ-follower.

He shouldn't be afraid of *trying* to win a contest just because he is a nice Christian. I don't know where that lie came from but it isn't biblical. The "nice guy syndrome" was covered well by John Eldredge in *Wild at Heart.* I won't repeat it. Instead I'll directly refer to the mighty benefits of healthy competition. A boy needs it. As a mother your urge is going to be to shield him from every failure and wounded heart, but he doesn't need that. He will never become a man if he knows mama is going to bail him out of everything.

Vince Lombardi famously said that "if winning isn't important, why do they keep score?" There's a measure of truth in that. The desire to live with excellence and strive with all the gifting that God has given him must be unleashed within a boy. That's not an excuse for a dad to live vicariously though his son's baseball games, but it does mean he should be demanding full effort with the goal of winning.

Paul wrote in 1 Corinthians 9:27 that he disciplined his body and made it his slave. Sports aren't any different, because if God gives all good things, and your son is good at sports, him doing them with fiery excellence should be a priority. It's worship just like everything else that glorifies God.

Encourage him to join athletics. Put him in something competitive, and if he's involved in a league that doesn't focus on winning, tell him to try to (unselfishly) outscore everyone. A fine line doth exist between harmful competitiveness and healthy competitiveness, so I would suggest you encourage him to get involved with Fellowship of Christian Athletes. Upwards is another good one, but their ministry is to younger kids. FCA has a terrific system of instruction that imparts Godly competitiveness on young men. An FCA camp is probably held not far from you, so you might look into enrolling him. FCA coaches and leaders are fine men who will make great role models for your son. If you are single mom, I can honestly think of no better positive masculine influence on your son than a coach, especially a Christ-exalting coach.

★ THE PHILOSOPHER

A Philosopher could be a great defender of the faith. If he's wrestled with the tough issues himself and is devoted to knowledge, try challenging him to enter the intellectual arena. It's a dogfight out there in the schools, and we need kids on the front lines who look and sound like their classmates while speaking the truth in love. They can't feel pressured to present their opinions in one particular manner (i.e.

obnoxious quoting of verses in science class) because that will only dull their mental blades.

I wrote earlier that telling him to stop doubting does more harm than good. Let me repeat it again: telling him to stop doubting does more harm than good. A smart kid like the Philosopher will see through any light-headed baloney that people feed him. He's a Philosopher for a reason, and that's because his baloney detector is finely tuned. He can be arrogant, but that doesn't mean he shouldn't be commended for intellectual curiosity. Try encouraging him to come up with the ten biggest problems he has with Christianity and then tell him you'll research them because you're curious about them yourself. That will be a major bridge-builder because he'll stop viewing you as a mind-numbed robot and might respect what you have to say. It will take effort, but everything worthwhile does. After you think you've found some good books relating to the subjects, read them yourself and then talk to him.

His first response will likely be defensiveness and condescension. Remember, according to him, nobody has ever been as smart as he is. Resist the urge to slap him (something my own precious mother did all but once) and engage. It could be a rocky path, but if he thinks you genuinely care about what he thinks, then he may mellow out some. Let him join debate teams and other organizations that encourage thought. If God grabs a hold of him, we're going to need kids in those places.

★ THE MOODY MUSICIAN

I'm not gonna lie, this kid will be tricky. His mood changes so often that you aren't going to have time to deploy an effective strategy. The Moody Musician could be encouraged in his craft. It doesn't have to be specifically Christian music that can be a good influence on his peers. If others are inspired to seek for answers by listening to his struggles, and he knows their musical world, give him a shot. Communicate to him that you want him to come to his own conclusions and then let him sort it out himself. Don't panic if he doesn't want to write praise songs. Some of the most profoundly spiritual songs I have ever listened to were written by bands that had no idea what they were doing. Again, the glory of God is written everywhere; how a person chooses to use the gift God gave them determines their condition before Him. If they come to a saving knowledge of Jesus Christ, then that gift can be put to use in the way God intended it. If they live like heathens, then the gift is a contaminated remnant of what it could have been, but it still is evidence of God.

As I said before, forbidding bands from their music selection based upon what you heard someone say is probably not going to get you anywhere. It's not mindless drivel to him; it's connecting on a level that other influences on his life aren't. Do some research, explain your concern to him, then give him a chance to defend it. Even following that process, regardless of whether you still decide to remove the questionable bands, will make him feel like you at least respect him. Moody Musicians whose parents followed that process have admitted to me that they understand why certain music isn't allowed, and even though they wish they could listen to it they at least have a clear understanding of the matter. They also don't think of God as some tyrannical killjoy.

It's likely that what the Musician is after is truth, and if he is writing a song about truth, then what he's actually seeking is Jesus. It takes time for him to learn a proper view of Christ. Until the day comes when you hear the opening to really chomp him with the Evangelism Shark, let him wail away at his imagined problems and search for the answer himself.

★ THE KNUCKLEHEAD

The Knucklehead might benefit from you giving him permission to goof off. Within reason, of course. He has an important role in showing his friends that knowing Jesus is fun and hilarious, so tell him that. Try not to force him to calm down and "shush" all the time. Let him go run it out, expend some energy, and then try to figure out a way to tie a truth into what he's doing. I understand that burning plastic items in the backyard may contain a lack of profoundly stimulating illustration material, so just keep your eye out for an opening (and his safety).

Laughter is so critically important for this boy to see that I almost can't overstate it. Any goofy event you see the youth group doing, such as Turkey Bowling or Coke Rocket Halo, is a great place for him to get his quota of it. You may not be the funniest person on earth but that doesn't mean you shouldn't make an effort to expose him to it.

Let me also caution you against writing off his interest in spiritual matters just because he doesn't display any surface level signs. During retreats or conversations this kid always surprises me with his depth of thought. Like I said, he's smart but usually doesn't act like it. When he *does* act like it, be ready to listen. He picks up far more than we tend to give him credit for.

★ THE GANGSTER

The most important part in dealing with Gangster is first contact, so approach him with the intent to show that you respect him. I'm not saying bow down to him; you're the adult. I'm recommending that you speak to him *like a man*. The Gangster may be the warrior who one day confronts dark places with the light of Christ. Tell him that. Affirm his toughness and tell him that he can channel it for Jesus. He has warrior written all over him and should be told so. A lot of the guys I know who have turned their lives around from gangs are using that inherent leadership ability to wage a different kind of battle. Try not to just feminize the Gangster with demands about loving-kindness; let him retain his tough edge. He needs to let the Holy Spirit break him into humility, but God may also use his personality to wage war in wicked arenas one day. King David was a rough man; don't misunderstand all of those gentle Psalms. He was broken and humble before the Lord, but he was black terror to his enemies on a battlefield. So we ought to be.

This particular kid might be really interested in something like 2 Samuel Chapter 23. If he sees all the war and fighting in Scripture, the possibility that he will show an interest in them increases accordingly. It would be a good conversation to have with him that violence for the sake of violence will bring unending ruin into his life. Selfish violence leads to destruction, but courageous attacks on Satan's strongholds require hardened men with obedient spirits. The answer to the gangster's problems, according to the feminized culture, is to emasculate him. The real Jesus doesn't want to remove his edge; just redirect it.

We had a gangster who showed up one Wednesday night for church who had a chip on his shoulder. He didn't believe in God and told me so. God slowly broke him down into submission over a long period of time, but it required much prayer and many conversations assuring him that seeking the Lord's mercy didn't mean becoming a girl. I know that sounds callous but it's the front lines. Mushy talk doesn't get us anywhere and it isn't required to communicate the love of Christ. Gangsters only understand the language they use day to day with each other so we, within obvious moral limits, ought to be speaking it.

★ THE MELTING POT

The Melting Pot's call of duty could be any combination of these. Just make sure you tell him that whatever he decides to do he needs to execute it with maximum effort. Let him try greatly and fail greatly, if need be, but let him find his call. As soon as he realizes that his identity is not found in trying to be one of the other guys, the warrior buried deep inside will burst forth. When you see that happen, regardless of how or when it surfaces, don't stuff it back down and order him to bake cookies.

Correct him if he's wrong, but talk to him like a man and not a boy. Instead of resentment he will feel as though he is respected; which, of course, is almost too important to overstate. Picture the process like the Incredible Hulk exploding out of Bruce Banner's chest. The intrinsic manhood that God put in him is just primed and waiting to come out.

If he knows Jesus and comes from a strict Christian family, oppressing him with too much religion and straightjacket spirituality will likely destroy his view of God. He's already confused about his own identity; he doesn't need confusion in his view of God. Watch out for a goody two-shoes religious attitude coming from him. His peers will not be swayed by his arrogant moral stands and he'll grow up a Pharisee. The most problems caused in church are not from heathens but from Pharisees.

What kind of specific areas can a parent work on in order to help change their son's attitude towards God?

Fathers, you are the most important person in your son's life. No one can set that young man up for greater victories or more ruthless defeats. He will try to be just like you even when he hates you. He admires you, even if you think there's nothing to admire. Be the warrior he learns from. Chase after Jesus like you would the sun's light. Walk with integrity. Love the Lord. Honor your lady. Defend the weak. It's never too late to start.

None of the great people of history that God used to work His purposes had a spotless record. King David is a towering figure in the history of mankind and he messed up in ways you and I probably never will. Since he repented and wanted to make things right, God still used him mightily all the days of his life. Your objective is for your son to look back one day and say to himself, "that man is my hero." He might never say it aloud, but if you do your job right, chances are he'll think it.

Mothers, if you've been abandoned or you're doing it on your own, don't lose heart. I know your son makes no sense to you. He's not supposed to. Get him around men in a church that are trustworthy. Let him go on the youth retreats. Put him in a sport. Affirm him in every way you can think of. Yes, that means sitting there and watching one of his videogames.

The same goes if you're household is intact. A boy wants the admiration of his mother. An ongoing joke in my family is that my mother never seems to find anything wrong with what I do and it frustrates my sister to death. I'm her firstborn baby boy, see, so naturally anything I do must be perfect. Don't confuse that with the "my kid can do no wrong" disease. I vividly remember spankings in my household, so there was no shortage of discipline. I simply received a lot of affirmation from her and it motivated me to do better.

Affirmation doesn't remove your role of authority; it strengthens it. Your objective is for him to look back on his years in your nest and remember the love *and* the compliments he received from you.

That's all I've got. Your son is different than every other son out there, so to dissect his personality completely through paper and ink is unreasonable. I would recommend that you figure out his personality type, do what you can to let him discover the call of duty on his own, and simply trust in the Lord. That may sound too simple, and I know as a parent you desperately want to see him get right with God, but I think you might be surprised at how successful a more hands-off approach can be. And of course by hands-off, I am referring to letting Christ's hands take the place of your hands. He knows how to give the boy the Call.

It also boils down, once again, to the language you use. Instead of a constant nagging tone, or an angry demand for church attendance, you might try a different approach. Do what the Lord did when He appeared to a simple farmer named Gideon. While Gideon was threshing wheat, minding his own business, the angel of the Lord greets him with, "The Lord is with you, oh valiant warrior!"

Gideon was pretty shocked. He was caught off guard and reacted with hesitation. But somewhere deep inside his soul a flame sparked. He probably didn't know why, but he stood a little bit taller at the words of his Commander. The Lord knew that instead of simply handing out an edict, Gideon would respond to an affirmation of his manhood.

If you frame the Christian faith in words that call a boy to manhood, he might start paying attention. Instead of saying, "Son, you need to read your Bible and stop complaining," you could say, "You ought to crack open 2 Samuel and read about the guy killing 800 enemy soldiers by himself in one day." Okay, so it's not the Sermon on the Mount. But it's *something*. And if he will listen to *something*, then he may listen to more. Guys who care nothing for long passages about grace and forgiveness might pay attention to the war stories. They have to *want* to pick up that never-used copy of Scripture to get anything out of it.

In Matthew 4:19 Jesus just walks up to Peter and Andrew, who were fishing in the sea, and basically says "You two, drop those nets and follow me." There's no "please" or "maybe" attached to it. They had no options. The General had just given an order. Generals tend to be pretty soft-spoken. They know there's no reason to shout because they're the General and people fall all over themselves to obey the orders when the General gives them. The General spoke to the fishermen and they obeyed without question. That's the Call of Duty.

APPENDIX
QUESTIONS FROM A MOM

Upon completion of this manuscript, an editor/mother informed me that it might be a good idea to have a special section at the end which included questions a mother might have. Some of what has been mentioned before will be included here, but my goal is to more thoroughly address some issues that didn't fit with the original topic of the narrative.

I did not set out to write a completely comprehensive book about the life of a teenage boy; the intent was to describe why they don't like coming to church anymore. I realize, however, that many of the day to day issues parents face relate directly to why boys don't like church or spirituality. The following is a list of questions that a mother asked me to include at the end.

You mentioned a lot about a boy's need for respect. How else does that relate to my son not wanting to come to church?

If he feels like every time he comes to church someone is determined to grind him down with rules and regulations, then it should surprise no one that he would rather just sleep in on Sunday morning. A boy is simply a younger version of a man (brilliant analysis, I know), so the things that make men frustrated can equally frustrate a boy.

The lack of respect a man gets from those around him, or his wife always telling him what to do without trusting him, eventually wears him out. If a boy walks into a church building and feels like no one there values his beliefs or opinions, or he gets scrutinized with arrogant eyes, then he will effectively tune out anything being said in there.

How about at home? As a mother or father, how do I affirm my son when he's around me?

As I mentioned in the chapter *Respect*, find the things he's good at and compliment him on them. It might not be the things that you want him to be good at. Regardless, there's something he's trying his hardest on that you need to be aware of. Enter his world, find what it is that he excels in, and build him up from there.

Eventually, he might be interested to try the things you would love to see him try. As long as he knows you respect him for who he is, he will be less likely to shrug you off.

The story about the sexually active 15-year-old really troubled me. How do I talk to my son about sex?

Openness and honesty at all times. Since the topic of sex is taboo in many churches, it does the family no good to ignore it home. There's some great material out there, such as books written by Josh McDowell, which deal with the need to talk frankly and openly with teenagers about sexuality. The worst thing the church is doing nowadays is ignoring sexuality, or worse, making it sound like it's a bad thing. The church is still viewed as the place where sex is not allowed or exists for procreation purposes only.

Emphasize again and again the positive aspects of sex, the truth that God created it for pleasure, and the fact that it can only be enjoyed to the fullest measure of its design by a husband and wife. I don't recommend sheltering your son by telling him sex isn't all it's cracked up to be … that would be false and he'll know it.

The idea that sex doesn't feel good outside of marriage is a lie; of course it does, or else no one would be doing it. The difference is that, as believers in Christ, we know that the committed relationship of husband and wife is the original design God had for sex and, therefore, doesn't carry the baggage and consequences that immoral sexual behavior does.

You may know this in your head, but your son doesn't, so it's up to you to instruct him in the proper way of viewing sex. I would suggest not hiding anything. If there's no father in the household, then find another man, in the church or elsewhere, who's responsible enough to give the boy a frank discussion about sex. A great place to start is the youth pastor, providing he agrees with this strategy. Chances are he does agree with it but feels intimidated by those in the church who would rather he ignored the topic of sex when teaching the teenagers.

Cliff Graham

Help me understand the development stages for a middle school boy and high school boy. Are the teen years similar to the terrible twos, where a child learns to walk and talk, opening up a whole new universe of independence?

Very much so. They have to challenge the structure in part to understand how they fit in it. With a two-year-old, they are told the oven is hot, but they won't really understand that until they burn their hand. "If you throw a temper tantrum, son, you will be spanked." Even though they are physically growing up, their mental level is a bit slower to maturity. Yes, your son really is that simplistic in his head sometimes. A teen can drive a car, earn money, and do all sorts of things beyond his parent's control. Many of them drink. When they turn 18, many of them look at porn and try cigarettes. Some of this is challenging the structure to see how they fit in. A lot of guys tell me that their junior and senior year of high school is a lot harder than the first year of college. The reason for this is because the pressure to drink and smoke is much higher in high school. Sometimes, regardless of whether a parent did everything right, a boy will need to learn lessons the hard way. Trust that the Lord is in control and continue to pray that he learns the lessons he needs to learn.

But he's my baby! How do I protect my son from harm and yet still allow him to be exposed to challenges?

Once more, let me get back to the need for respect in a boy. It's all-powerful when it comes to forming his worldview.

A mom can hopelessly squelch a boy's self confidence when she is constantly fearful or overprotective. There is certainly a line, but as long as it's not too physically dangerous try letting him out once in a while.

Exposing him to something that will challenge him could be as simple as letting him go on the youth retreat to the mountains or going to the inner city with a missions group. Don't hide him away from the world.

The "danger" you fear might be a spiritual one, such as protecting him from harmful influences. I presented in the book the reasons why this is a destructive attitude. You can't protect him forever, and what use is he when he gets on the outside of your house and runs in fear of Lost People? That's not what Jesus wants Christians to do. He warned us against being "bad salt" in Matthew 5:13. We need to be "in the world and not of the world" according to John 17. Worrying too much about your son is the equivalent of you saying to God, "Lord, I know you can't watch over my son, so allow me to do your job for you."

Your son is being groomed for battle while he lives in your household. What good is he on a battlefield when he's never been trained to fight? The more you sweat in peacetime, the less you bleed in war, as the old saying goes.

How does the relationship between a mother and father impact a boy's view of God?

If a boy sees that his mother doesn't respect his father, regardless of how much of a bum he may be, then he will automatically assume that he is doomed to the same fate. His wife will never respect him, etc. A boy needs role models to look up to and imitate, and if his father is not a positive influence, then she needs to let him be around other guys and their struggles. I'm in no way saying she should subvert the father's authority, but I do believe that a good youth pastor or athletic coach can fill a part of the void. Timothy in the Bible had no earthly father's influence that we know of, but God provided one in the form of Paul. Everything is about influence, *everything*. He will remember only a few things you ever said with your mouth; he will remember everything about your influence. He'll recall the influence of a really great youth pastor or man in the church who treated him "like a man" and told him what the Call of Duty was.

You mentioned some ways that the church fails in preparing young men for the world. What are some things we can do to change that?

The church tends to think that by simply presenting Bible stories a teenager is sufficiently prepared to face the world. I cannot disagree more with that mindset, however well-intentioned it may be. The issue is not the sufficiency of the Word of God. It doesn't matter how many verses you know when you're sitting in science class trying to argue evolution; or trying to explain to a lost friend why sex outside of marriage is bad when the guy keeps saying how good it feels. The church crams a lot of Bible verses in their heads and never really gets to the practical application of them.

You can use the Bible as your basis and discuss other issues relevant to young people. One series of lessons we did, and had great success with, involved exploring the different types of music that they were listening to. Nothing was played during our sessions that was inappropriate, but we wanted the kids to listen to how the world viewed belief in Christ. The goal was for them to be better prepared to have a relevant discussion with their peers. Be creative. Experiment some. Don't confine your discussion about spiritual matters to Scriptural exposition. That's not to say we do away with learning Scripture, but teach it in a way that is understandable to teenagers where they are at. Paul at the Aeropagus did the very same thing.

Doesn't telling a boy about "war" encourage him to be violent?

Absolutely. He *needs* to be violent, though not in the way you may be afraid of. I'm not referring to selfish lust for death. I'm saying that he needs to be violent in the way he attacks his calling in life. Violent in the way he deals with hardship. Violent in the way he follows Jesus. What do I mean by violent? Completely devoted *to the point of death*. I realize using the word violent can be abrasive, but I don't know of any other way to describe the intensity of the concept. The Greek word used for violence is *biazo*, and Strong's translates it as "to use force." It doesn't simply imply killing or death. We need to be forceful in our obedience to the calling on our lives. Following Jesus needs to be something more than just logging church time; a young man needs to have a mindset that he will have to give everything he's made of to follow Him. Using war language and war symbolism is exactly what the writers of Scripture did, so I think we ought to do the same.

As I have said before, I really believe that the emphasis on love and mercy has an important place; the problem is that it has become the *only* focus the church seems to have in recent times. Moderation, obviously, needs to be taught. So does love and compassion. But I think those are already overly emphasized, hence the reason we see so much apathy. It's time to bring back the warrior mentality. The Spartans trained their young from an early age to live in a constant state of battle. The nation of Israel has always had to function in the full knowledge that war could break out at any moment. Not a bad idea. (Although hanging out is important, too.)

CPSIA information can be obtained at www.ICGtesting.com
Printed in the USA
LVOW11s0904160615

442629LV00001B/46/P